STAR WARS
ABSOLUTELY EVERYTHING YOU NEED TO KNOW

Written by
ADAM BRAY,
KERRIE DOUGHERTY,
COLE HORTON,
AND MICHAEL KOGGE

CONTENTS

Where does **Ezra** have to face **nine difficult** and **scary** Jedi Trials?

PROTECTORS OF THE GALAXY

Whose starship does **R2-D2 save** from certain **destruction**?

4

CHAPTER 1

What **nickname** is the young **Luke Skywalker** given on Tatooine?

JEDI OF THE REPUBLIC

"KOH-TO-YAH!"
"GREETINGS!"
In Kel Dor, the language of Plo Koon's people.

Q: So what *is* a Jedi?
A: A **protector** and **peacekeeper**—the good guy who upholds **justice** and **keeps harmony** in the galaxy (**or tries to**... it's not easy!). The Jedi do this by using the **Force**, a **powerful energy** coursing through every living thing in the galaxy. Jedi also use the Force to **defend** themselves, but it has a **dark side**, too...

In numbers

1,000 generations
The length of time the Jedi have been the guardians of peace throughout the galaxy.

PLO KOON
Kel Dor from Dorin • Jedi Master and General • Frequently undertakes dangerous missions

YARAEL POOF
Quermian from Quermia • Jedi Master • Expert at Jedi mind tricks and illusions

Q: Why does Plo Koon wear a breath mask and goggles?
A: Oxygen is **poisonous** to Plo Koon's species, the Kel Dor. Koon's breath mask **filters** the air on Coruscant, while his goggles **protect his eye fluids** from evaporating!

ADI GALLIA
Tholothian from Coruscant • Uses Form V lightsaber combat • Great starfighter pilot

Yarael Poof has **TWO BRAINS**—one in his **HEAD** and the second in his **CHEST**.

Adi Gallia joins Obi-Wan Kenobi on his **VITAL** mission in the Outer Rim to **FIND AND STOP** the evil Darth Maul and Savage Opress.

How did Even Piell receive the **SCAR** on his face? The scar is an old **BATTLE WOUND** that he carries as a badge of honor.

MACE WINDU
Human from Haruun Kal • Jedi Master, Master of the Order • The Council's greatest battlefield General and warrior

YADDLE
Jedi Master • Same mysterious species as Yoda • Skilled in little-known Jedi powers • Highly sought after for her great wisdom

COOL!!
As a senior Council member, Mace Windu makes sure his **VOICE IS HEARD**—both in noisy negotiations *and* with his **UNIQUE AMETHYST-BLADED** lightsaber!

EVEN PIELL
Lannik from planet Lannik • Jedi Master • Revered for courage and telekinesis powers • Enhanced hearing thanks to large ears

STRANGE

...BUT TRUE
Yaddle is only **half the age** of Yoda, but still **more than 400** years old.

8

Fast Facts

LEADER: Master of the Order, elected by a unanimous vote of the Council's members

HOMEWORLD: Coruscant

AFFILIATION: Galactic Republic

AIM: To serve the will of the Force, to train new Jedi

WOW!...

10,000

The number of Jedi Knights in the Order

COUNCIL CHAMBER

Located in Jedi Temple • 12 customized chairs ring a fern-patterned floor • Stunning bird's-eye views over the city of Coruscant

KI-ADI-MUNDI
Cerean from Cerea • Jedi Master and General • Lightsaber expert • Leader of the Galactic Marine clone troopers

SAESEE TIIN
Iktotchi from Iktotch • Jedi Master and General • Ace starfighter pilot • Natural superior telepathic powers

Saesee Tiin's **HORNS** will **GROW BACK** if damaged!

REALLY?!
The **COMPLEX BRAIN** inside Ki-Adi-Mundi's long, **CONE-SHAPED HEAD** relies on **BLOOD PUMPED** from his **TWO HEARTS!**

"We're keepers of peace, not soldiers."
MACE WINDU

Peek behind the scenes
Episode I originally featured a puppet version of Yoda. In later releases, George Lucas substituted a more polished digital version, to give Yoda a consistent appearance throughout the prequel trilogy.

HEAD HONCHOS

Who **rules** the Jedi **roost**? Only twelve of the wisest and finest Jedi Masters get to sit on the **High Council.** These noble leaders keep the Jedi Order **out of trouble,** maintain **balance in the Force,** and **handpick future Jedi stars.**

YODA
Jedi Master, Grand Master, Master of the Order • Famous teacher • Perhaps the greatest Master of the Force ever

9

Fast Facts

HOMEWORLD: Tatooine

AFFILIATION: Jedi Order and the Republic

ABILITIES: Expert pilot, superior Force abilities, talented mechanic, speaks Huttese

OCCUPATION: Slave, podracer pilot, Jedi Padawan, later Knight

SPECIES: Human

REALLY?!
Young Anakin has a **TRANSMITTER CHIP** hidden inside his body. If he tries to sneak away from Watto, he could be **BLOWN UP!**

Q: What are midi-chlorians?

A: Midi-chlorians are **tiny, intelligent life-forms** that live inside the cells of **all living things** in the galaxy. They do no harm, and help their host **use the Force**. The **more** midi-chlorians someone has, the **more powerful** a Jedi they may become.

MECHANICAL MASTER
Anakin has always had a talent for engineering. He enjoys **tinkering** with **podracers** and **droids** as a boy, and graduates to **starfighters** and his new **prosthetic arm** as an adult!

UNHAPPY ENDINGS
All of Anakin's relationships seem to **end in sadness**—especially with the women closest to him.

• **Shmi Skywalker**
Anakin's kind, loving mother, Shmi, is **taken captive** by Tusken Raiders. When she **dies** in their camp, Anakin is **devastated**.

• **Padmé Amidala**
After falling **in love**, Anakin and Senator Amidala **secretly marry** on Naboo. In a tragic turn of events, Padmé **perishes during childbirth**.

• **Ahsoka Tano**
Ahsoka is Anakin's **Padawan** during the Clone Wars. He is distressed when she **leaves** the Jedi Order.

• **Princess Leia Organa**
Anakin does not meet his **daughter**, Leia, until he becomes Darth Vader. He doesn't even **realize** that she *is* his daughter until it is far **too late!**

THE MAVERICK

Rescued from **slavery** and squalor by the **Jedi**, Anakin Skywalker quickly rises to the rank of **Knight**. His Force potential is **so strong** that some Jedi believe he will **save the galaxy** from darkness. But things don't go quite as expected...!

Timeline

23 years old—joins the Jedi Council, but is caught between loyalty to the Jedi and his friend Chancellor Palpatine; becomes Darth Vader.

20 years old—marries Padmé Amidala; fights for Republic as a general during the Clone Wars.

14 years old—builds first lightsaber on Ilum; trains with Obi-Wan Kenobi on Coruscant.

10 years old—is accepted into the Jedi Order as a gifted youngling.

9 years old—is discovered on Tatooine by Jedi Master Qui-Gon Jinn; wins Boonta Eve podrace.

3 years old—slave owner Watto wins Anakin from Gardulla the Hutt.

You know you're strong with the Force if you can...

1. Perform astonishing, circus-worthy acrobatics.
2. Move objects without touching them.
3. Speak with some people using only your mind.
4. See visions of the future (although this is a troubling ability that may lead to the dark side!).

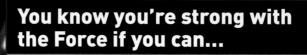

"Not again! Obi-Wan's gonna kill me."

Anakin is very unlucky with **lightsabers!** He **drops** his Padawan blade during a mission, which Obi-Wan returns (with a telling off), only for Anakin to accidentally **destroy** it in a droid factory! Anakin's **replacement** lightsaber is then taken and kept by Obi-Wan after he wins their epic duel on Mustafar. Decades later the Jedi finally hands it to Anakin's **son, Luke.**

"Next time, try not to lose it… This weapon is your life."

OBI-WAN TO ANAKIN

Anakin is trained by a line of **unusually independent** Jedi. **Count Dooku's stubborn** ways are a strong influence on his apprentice **Qui-Gon,** who pushes for Anakin to be trained as a Jedi. Could Dooku's teachings be an influence on Anakin's **dark future**?

In numbers

700kph (435mph)
The maximum speed of Anakin's ship, the *Twilight*

105m (344ft 6in)
The maximum altitude Anakin's podracer can fly

15 min 42 sec
Anakin's winning time in the Boonta Eve Classic podrace

2 witnesses
Attend the wedding of Anakin and Padmé—R2-D2 and C-3PO

1.85m (6ft 1in)
Anakin's adult height

Tell me more!

LIFE AS A SLAVE

Anakin's mother, Shmi Skywalker, is **captured by pirates** and sold into **slavery** when she is just a girl. She and Anakin end up as the property of **Gardulla the Hutt** on Tatooine. Later, a Toydarian **junk-dealer** named **Watto** wins them both in a **bet** with Gardulla.

"Someday I will be the most powerful Jedi ever!"
ANAKIN SKYWALKER

Peek behind the scenes
Colin Hanks, Paul Walker, and Ryan Phillippe all auditioned for the part of Anakin Skywalker, but the role was given to Hayden Christensen.

WOW!...

20,000+

Anakin's midi-chlorian count per cell (the highest ever recorded)

REALLY?!
Obi-Wan **CHOPS DARTH MAUL IN HALF** on Naboo. The Sith survives and vows revenge on the Jedi!

Q: Why is Obi-Wan called "Ben" on Tatooine?
A: Obi-Wan uses his **old nickname** so that he won't be found by the Empire, which is **hunting down** Jedi survivors after the Clone Wars.

THE MENTOR

Obi-Wan Kenobi is a **noble knight, skilled swordsman**, and **nifty negotiator**, who serves as **Jedi Master** for **Anakin Skywalker**. As one of the few remaining Jedi during the dark times of the Empire's rule, he also **mentors Luke Skywalker** in the ways of the Force.

Obi-Wan's droid, R4-P17, is cut apart by buzz droids during a space battle.

Peek behind the scenes
Creator George Lucas named Obi-Wan's homeworld "Stewjon" after talk show host John Stewart.

Love interest...
Obi-Wan falls in love with Satine Kryze, Duchess of Mandalore, but the Jedi code forbids attachment!

In numbers

212th
The Attack Battalion led by Obi-Wan

145cm (4ft 9in)
Length of Obi-Wan's lightsaber blade

19 years
Spent in hiding from the Empire

1.82m (6ft)
Obi-Wan's height

Fast Facts

OCCUPATION:
Jedi Master

AFFILIATION:
The Jedi Order

ABILITIES: Jedi mind tricks, lightsaber combat, negotiation

LEAST FAVORITE JOB:
Flying

12

Clone Commander Cody **betrays** Obi-Wan and tries to destroy him when Palpatine issues **Order 66**, the execution of Jedi. Obi-Wan is caught in the trap, but he manages to **escape**!

"Help me Obi-Wan Kenobi, you're my only hope."
PRINCESS LEIA

Obi-Wan **lectures** Anakin about **never losing** his lightsaber, but Obi-Wan has lost his own lightsaber **many times**!

Q: How does Obi-Wan reappear after Darth Vader defeats him?

A: After being **struck down** by Darth Vader on the Death Star, Obi-Wan becomes **one with the Force**. He appears as a **Force spirit** and is able to communicate with Luke and Yoda.

OBI-WAN'S HERMIT HUT

Small home on Tatooine • Hermit hideout for a wanted Jedi • 136km (85 miles) from the Lars homestead, to keep watch on Luke Skywalker

NO WAY!!
Obi-Wan once **FELL** into a **NEST** of nasty **GUNDARKS** and was saved by Anakin!

At the end of an **epic fight** between Obi-Wan and cyborg Separatist leader General Grievous, both combatants **lose** their lightsabers, and Obi-Wan is **forced to use his blaster** to eliminate his enemy. He then discards the **"uncivilized" weapon** in disgust!

"Well, I don't know anyone named Obi-Wan, but old Ben lives out beyond the Dune Sea."
LUKE SKYWALKER

STRANGE

...BUT TRUE
Jedi General Obi-Wan once wore **Mandalorian armor and a jetpack**! It was a **disguise** to infiltrate the Mandalorian capital and **save** Duchess Satine from Darth Maul!

Fast Facts

OCCUPATION: Jedi Padawan, Jedi Knight

AFFILIATION: Jedi Order during Clone Wars, later joining the first rebels

HOMEWORLD: Unknown

SPECIES: Togruta

ABILITIES: Strong leader, quick reflexes

FREE AGENT

The Clone Wars make headstrong Ahsoka Tano a Jedi legend —until she realizes her destiny may not lie with the Jedi at all. It may lie, as it so often has, in her own hands... and heart.

"You're stuck with me, Skyguy."
AHSOKA TO ANAKIN SKYWALKER

Ahsoka wields her lightsaber in a **REVERSE GRIP**, to accord with the ancient **SHIEN** style of Jedi combat.

COOL!!

Because her species has **NO HAIR**, Ahsoka weaves her Padawan braid out of **SILKA BEADS**!

Peek behind the scenes
The Clone Wars producers hired a martial artist to model Ahsoka's acrobatic moves so that they could be realistically animated using computer graphics.

A REBEL HEART TAKES HER OWN PATH

Fearless and fiery, Ahsoka relies on her **instincts** as much as her **Jedi skills**. Even as Anakin's Padawan, she rushes **headfirst into danger**.

Falsely accused of **blowing up** the **Jedi Temple** and almost expelled, Ahsoka loses respect for the Order. She leaves the Jedi to **create her own destiny**.

Her **bumpy path to Jedi Knighthood** also shows Ahsoka that **planning** and **patience** are as vital as courage—lessons that come in handy on her solo missions.

A **wiser but no less gutsy** Ahsoka reveals her identity as **Fulcrum**, the shadowy figure **helping the rebels** fight the Empire on Lothal.

14

WOW!...

25

The echolocation distance Ahsoka can detect with her hollow montral horns in meters (82 feet)

WHO TRAINED WHOM?

Ahsoka shares Anakin's **rebellious streak**, just as Anakin does of his **Jedi Master** Obi-Wan Kenobi. In this way, the teachings and legacy of **Qui-Gon Jinn** live on.

QUI-GON JINN   OBI-WAN KENOBI   ANAKIN SKYWALKER   AHSOKA TANO

TOP 5

NICKNAMES

Ahsoka loves giving her friends and enemies silly monikers.
1. **"Skyguy"**—Anakin Skywalker
2. **"Stinky"**—Rotta the Hutt (Jabba's infant son)
3. **"Goldie"**—astromech R3-S6
4. **"Grumpy"**—General Grievous
5. **"Artooie"**—R2-D2

Not to be left out, Anakin has his own nickname for Ahsoka— **"Snips"**—because of her snippy, lively personality!

Tell me more!

THE LIFE CHANGING MEETING

Jedi Master Plo Koon discovers the toddler Ahsoka's **sensitivities to the Force** while on a mission. He brings her to the Jedi Temple on Coruscant to be trained, and **maintains a strong bond** with her throughout her Padawan years.

In numbers

14 years old
Age when Ahsoka is apprenticed to Anakin Skywalker

3 years old
Ahsoka's age when she is found by Plo Koon and taken to join the Jedi Order

2 years
Time spent as Anakin's Padawan trainee

1.88m (6ft 1in)
Ahsoka's adult height

DON'T UPSET THIS DROID...
What's Ahsoka's **most vital** equipment on board her Delta-7B Jedi starfighter? Her **aggressive** astromech droid R7-A7! He plots hyperspace routes and repairs her Delta-7B *Aethersprite*-class light interceptor when needed.

A CLOSER LOOK

TOP 7 SUCCESSFUL MISSIONS

1. Helps save Jabba the Hutt's son.
2. Liberates her fellow Togruta who were enslaved.
3. Breaks the Separatist blockade of Ryloth.
4. Halts the spread of the Blue Shadow Virus.
5. Rescues Baron Papanoida's daughters.
6. Stops bounty hunter Aurra Sing from slaying Senator Amidala.
7. Exposes the Mandalorian Prime Minister's corruption.

BEST KNOWN FOR

WISECRACKS AND SNARKY WIT

Ahsoka Tano

REALLY?!

Reckless Ahsoka makes unlikely friends with the most trusted of Padawans, Barriss Offee, who's **NOT AS LOYAL** as she seems...

> "When nine hundred years you reach, look as good, you will not."
> **YODA TO LUKE SKYWALKER**

REALLY?!
Yoda learns how to **SURVIVE** as a **FORCE SPIRIT AFTER DEATH** from the late Qui-Gon Jinn. He then teaches this **SECRET** to both Obi-Wan Kenobi and Anakin Skywalker.

When Yoda first hears the voice of Qui-Gon Jinn's **Force spirit**, he thinks he's having a **hallucination** and has a full **medical checkup**!

How to talk like Yoda

Yoda speaks Basic in the phrasing of his native language, which can sound a little strange.

"HELP YOU, I CAN."

"POWERFUL, YOU HAVE BECOME."

"WHAT KNOW YOU OF READY?"

"TRULY WONDERFUL, THE MIND OF A CHILD IS."

Yoda's feet are like those of many **birds**, with **three toes** at the **front** and **one** at the **back**.

Peek behind the scenes

Yoda's face takes inspiration, in part, from two **real-life faces**. Working from a design by Joe Johnston, sculptor Stuart Freeborn used his own face—and Einstein's!

In numbers

20,000 Jedi
The estimated number that Yoda has trained over his lifetime

900 years
Yoda's age

800 years
How long Yoda has been training Jedi

23 years
Period of Yoda's exile on Dagobah

Fast Facts

HOMEWORLD: Unknown

SPECIES: Unknown

AFFILIATION: Jedi Order, Galactic Republic

JEDI RANK: Grand Master of the Jedi Order (leads Council)

REPUBLIC ARMY RANK: General

DISLIKES: Luke's rebel pilot food rations (he spits them out!)

Q: Why is Yoda unsure about young Anakin Skywalker?

A: Yoda senses **strong anger in Anakin**. **Rage and fear** can make a Jedi turn to the **dark side of the Force** and Yoda is worried that this may happen to Anakin. Much to his regret, he turns out to be right!

16

TOP 5

YODA'S WIT AND WISDOM

1. Do, or do not. There is no try.
2. Size matters not... judge me by my size, do you?
3. My ally is the Force, and a powerful ally it is.
4. Excitement. Heh. Adventure. Hah. A Jedi craves not these things.
5. Always pass on what you have learned.

Mind the furniture! Yoda confronts evil enemy Darth Sidious in a **ferocious lightsaber duel** that includes **Force-throwing huge Senate pods at each other** inside the Senate chamber!

Tell me more!

HOW TO MASTER THE FORCE

Don't let his small size or quirky manner fool you—Yoda is one of the **most powerful and respected** Jedi in history. As well as his **formidable fighting skills**, he is a **brave** and **wise** general. Yoda's deep connection to the Force makes him a **gifted teacher** and **philosopher**, who always seeks to understand the Force better.

THE JEDI LEGEND

Yoda's history may be **shrouded in mystery**, but there's nothing uncertain about the ancient Jedi Master's **legendary Force power** and **lightsaber combat expertise**—especially to his unlucky foes.

Yoda may be in **exile** on Dagobah, but he still uses the Force to **watch over and advise** surviving Jedi like Kanan Jarrus and his Padawan, Ezra.

Q: Why does Yoda give Anakin a Padawan?

A: Yoda knows Anakin still carries many fears and cannot let go of his **tragic past**. He hopes that by **teaching the Padawan Ahsoka Tano**, the young Jedi will learn that he does not need to be **so protective** of those who he loves.

NOT JUST A STICK

Yoda's walking cane, made from a **gimer** stick, symbolizes a Jedi Master's **ancient wisdom**. But it's not just a status symbol—when Yoda **chews** on the gimer bark it releases natural plant substances that help him **meditate**. Plus, the nutritious juice inside **eases thirst** and acts as a **natural painkiller!**

YODA'S TOP 4 JEDI ABILITIES

1. Master of all lightsaber fighting styles.
2. Ability to sense the future.
3. Impressive levitation capabilities.
4. Can deflect Force lightning with his hands.

Yoda's Dagobah home is not just built of mud and stones. It also includes **pieces of the escape pod** that secretly brought him to the planet.

Peek behind the scenes

An early design for Yoda became the model for Yaddle, a female of Yoda's species who sits on the Jedi High Council during the Naboo Crisis.

FAN FACT

Originally, photos were taken of a **monkey** in a robe with a **cane** and a **mask**, to see if that would work to play Yoda.

CLONE TROOPERS AND COMMANDERS

WOW!...

192,000

Clone troopers present at the Battle of Geonosis

When plans backfire!

Commander Gree receives Order 66 during the Battle of Kashyyyk and **tries to eliminate Yoda.** But sensing betrayal, the Jedi draws his lightsaber just in time, and **Gree loses his own head instead!**

SUPER TROOPERS

Peek behind the scenes

In Episodes II and III, actor Temuera Morrison wore a blue **bodysuit to play troopers** Cody, Odd Ball, and Jag. The suit was later digitally replaced with computer-generated clone armor.

Q: Who asks for this huge army to be made?

A: Sifo-Dyas, a Jedi High Council member who senses **a looming galactic war** and tasks the Kaminoans to create a clone army for the Republic. When the Sith learn of this, they **murder Sifo-Dyas** so they can **control** the clones' creation.

Tell me more!

SILENCING YOUR ENEMIES

When Chancellor Palpatine's **true identity** as Sith Lord Darth Sidious is discovered, he issues **Order 66**, telling all clone troopers that the **Jedi** have betrayed the Republic and **must be eliminated immediately!**

BEST KNOWN FOR
TRYING TO BUMP OFF OBI-WAN (UNDER ORDER 66)
Commander Cody

Bred in their millions, these identical, loyal, and relentless clone soldiers of the Republic are the future of galactic warfare. But they also come with a lethal secret—a command code to make them destroy their Jedi officers!

TOP 5

CLONE COMMANDERS

1. **CAPTAIN REX (CT-7567)**—Reports to Jedi Anakin Skywalker. **Mentor and friend** of Jedi Padawan Ahsoka Tano.

2. **COMMANDER CODY (CC-2224)**—Reports to Jedi Master Obi-Wan Kenobi. **Close friend** of Obi-Wan and Captain Rex.

3. **WOLFFE (CC-3636)**—Reports to Jedi Master Plo Koon. Commands the famous "Wolf Pack" Battalion.

4. **COMMANDER FOX (CC-1010)**—Reports to Chancellor Palpatine. **Rescues** Padmé Amidala and **arrests** Ziro the Hutt.

5. **COMMANDER GREE (CC-1004)**—Reports to Jedi Master Luminara Unduli. Named after a **tentacled alien species.**

Clone Lieutenant

"No clone uses their number. I am Fives. Call me Fives."
FIVES TO AZI-3 ON KAMINO

Commander Deviss

STRANGE

...BUT TRUE

Count Dooku secretly orders the Kaminoans to put **computer chips in the brains** of every clone trooper, which makes them **obey Palpatine** without question.

Just following orders

Clone Commander Fox arrests Padawan Ahsoka Tano when she is **wrongly blamed for bombing the Jedi Temple.** He also destroys clone trooper Fives, who has been **falsely accused of trying to harm Chancellor Palpatine.**

Clone Commander

Traitors in the ranks

Some clones don't follow orders. Jedi General Pong Krell **plans to execute Fives and Jesse** for disobedience, but when Captain Rex learns **Krell is a traitor,** he arrests the Jedi. Ultimately, clone trooper Dogma slays Krell himself.

REALLY?!

Echo fights alongside teammates **Heavy, Cutup, Fives, and Droidbait.** When Captain Rex slaps his hand, covered in **BLUE EEL BLOOD,** on Echo's armor, the mark becomes **Echo's symbol!**

In numbers

80kg (176lbs)
Average clone trooper weight

13 years
Clone service time from the first clone birth to the founding of the Empire

10 years old
Age when clones are combat-ready

2+ x
Growth rate of clones compared to normal people

Fast Facts

AFFILIATION: Galactic Republic

LEADER: Supreme Chancellor Palpatine

CLAIM TO FAME: The devastating galaxy-wide conflict known as the **Clone Wars** is named after them

ARMED AND DANGEROUS

During the **Clone Wars**, the Republic builds a **formidable arsenal**. These **vehicles and weapons** trigger the transformation of the **peaceful Republic** into the **invincible military machine** that is the **Empire!**

BEST KNOWN FOR

WITHSTANDING SUB-ZERO TEMPERATURES

CK-6 swoop bikes

Q: How do clone soldiers enter a combat zone?

A: They ride to a planet's surface in either heavily armed *Acclamator*-class **assault ships** or smaller, but lethal, **assault gunships**.

DC-15 BLASTER RIFLE

EMP PULSE GRENADE

DC-17 BLASTER PISTOL

In numbers ● ● ●

700 crew members
Required to operate *Acclamator*-class assault ships

99.71m (327ft)
Length of the Republic's experimental stealth ship

66
Secret clone order number given to execute all Jedi

4.15kg (9lbs 2oz)
Weight of DC-15A blaster rifle

1.83m (6ft)
Height of a clone trooper

TOP 4

CLONE TROOPER WEAPONS
1. **DC-15 blaster rifle**—standard issue long-range weapon with 500 shot capacity.
2. **DC-15a blaster**—smaller weapon with 500 shots, but a shorter range.
3. **DC-17 blaster pistol**—ideal for close combat, 50 shot capacity.
4. **EMP pulse grenade**—electromagnetic emission disables battle droids' circuits.

STRANGE

...BUT TRUE
The **cloaking device** on the Republic's radical new **stealth ship** makes the vessel **invisible to scanners**—and even the **human eye!** Blink and you'll miss it!

DC-15A BLASTER

TETH

Planet of jungles and flat-topped mountains • Site of revered B'omarr monastery, turned Separatist fortress • Testing ground for new clone vehicles and weaponry during Battle of Teth

"Teth? That's Wild Space. The droid army isn't even in that sector."
ANAKIN SKYWALKER

The Republic's stun tanks bring down not only Separatist WARSHIPS, but also the fearsome ZILLO BEAST!

Peek behind the scenes
The clone trooper DC-15 blaster rifle is based on the design of the German MG 34 machine gun from World War II.

REALLY?!
The turbo tank's TEN wheels and COCKPIT AT EACH END allow this war machine to make quick turns.

AT-TE

AT-AP

AT-RT

WOW!...

1.137

Length of a Republic *Venator*-class Star Destroyer in kilometers (3,730 feet)

TOP 3

REPUBLIC WALKERS
1. **AT-TE**—six-legged walker able to carry troops and climb steep slopes.
2. **AT-RT**—reconnaissance walker built for speed and maneuverability.
3. **AT-AP**—three-legged "pod walker" used for long-range artillery attacks.

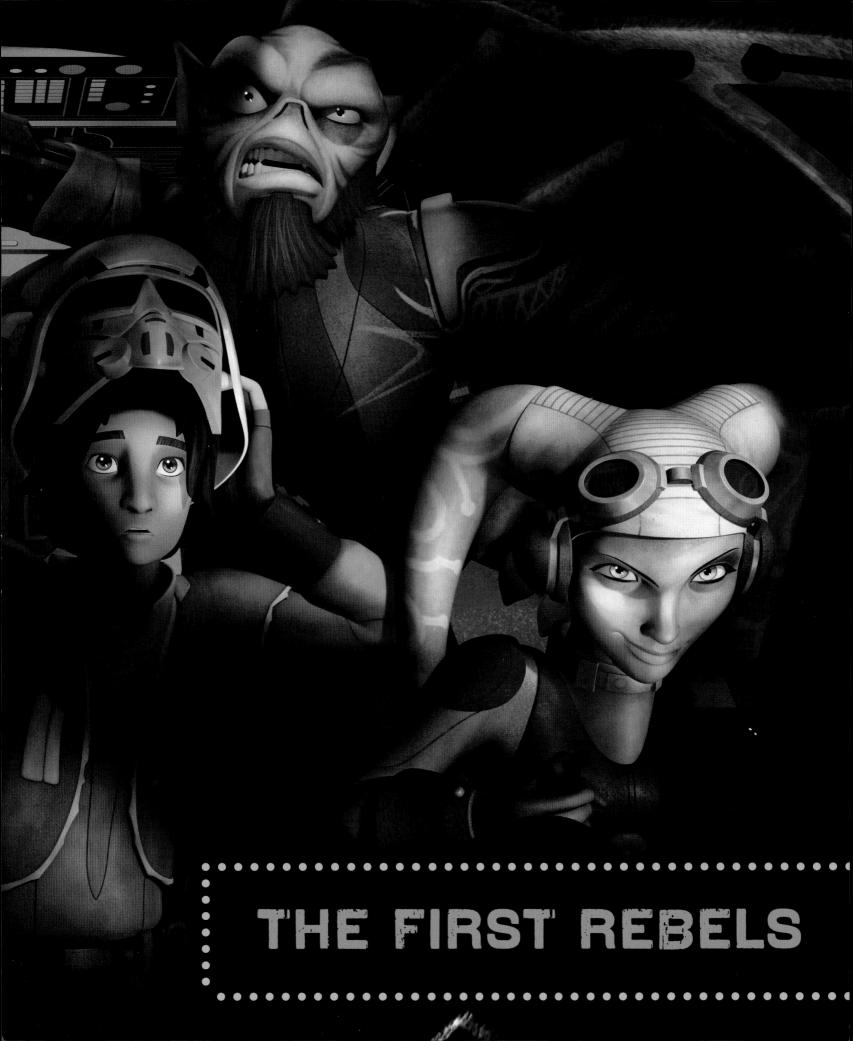

THE FIRST REBELS

Fast Facts

OCCUPATION: Starship captain, rebellion starter

SPECIES: Twi'lek

HOMEWORLD: Ryloth

ABILITIES: Makes flying the *Ghost* look easy, charismatic leader

Q: Who is "Fulcrum"?

A: Fulcrum is the codename for Hera's **mysterious contact** who gives **advice, missions, and aid** to the team. Imagine the rebels' surprise when it turns out to be the Jedi rebel **Ahsoka Tano**!

Top 5

Ways to be a great rebel leader

1 **HONE YOUR FLYING SKILLS** Fly fast to escape a squad of enemy TIE fighters when the *Ghost*'s shields fail.

2 **BE READY FOR ANYTHING** Fight off a flurry of fyrnocks on an abandoned clone trooper asteroid base.

3 **LOOK AFTER YOUR TEAM** Rescue your crewmates from a well-guarded Imperial communications tower.

4 **BREAK THE RULES!** Disobey your rebel contact's orders and lead a mission to save co-leader Kanan.

5 **BE A TALENT-SPOTTER** Convince Kanan to train Ezra—the boy has talent!

> "Do I have to do *everything* myself?"
> **HERA**

HOW TO GESTURE WITH LEKKU

Hera's species has developed a unique sign language using their lekku. They can communicate without saying a single word!

"HELLO."
RIGHT LEK TIP RAISED

"GOODBYE."
LEFT LEK TIP DIPPED

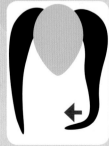

"LOVE YOU."
BOTH LEKKU TIPS CROSSED OVER, TWICE

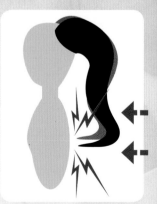

"MAY SPICE SALT YOUR WOUNDS!"
BOTH LEKKU TIPS JABBED INTO SPEAKER'S BACK

26

BEST KNOWN FOR

MAKING ENEMY PILOTS SPACESICK

Hera

TOP 4 FAVORITE LOCATIONS
1. Hurtling through hyperspace.
2. The pilot's chair of the *Ghost*.
3. A big field in Lothal's grasslands to land.
4. Old Jho's Pit Stop for snacks and swapping tips with fellow pilots.

Tricks to escape pursuit
- Drop a cargo container, **like a missile**, onto an enemy target.
- Dodge Imperial sensors by switching onboard systems to **"silent mode."**
- Hide from a Star Destroyer by **attaching** your freighter to **its underbelly**.
- Get a crew member to **blow up something** to create a diversion.

STRANGE

...BUT TRUE
Hera's father and greatest inspiration, **Cham Syndulla**, is a reluctant Twi'lek hero. His leadership of the **resistance on Ryloth** against the Separatists is **celebrated in song.**

Peek behind the scenes

Hera wasn't a tall Twi'lek in the early design stages of *Rebels*—she started out as a short, motherly woman.

TRUE BELIEVER

In numbers

5,929 Twi'leks
Of the Syndulla clan taken as Hutt slaves

24 years old
Hera's age

2 head-tails
On each Twi'lek

1.76m (5ft 9in)
Hera's height

Spectre 2
Hera's rebel codename

Don't just call Hera Syndulla an expert pilot— she's the **gutsy captain** of a **motley rebel gang** on Lothal. Her belief in battling evil and her wise strategies help hold this **family of misfits together!**

Tell me more!

WHAT ARE TWI'LEK TENTACLES FOR?
The **two long tentacles** that grow from Hera's skull are known as **lekku**, or head-tails. Super-sensitive lekku can **grab and hold things** and react to the slightest touch. **Never mess with them**—a damaged lek can cause **serious harm** to a Twi'lek's health.

27

Fast Facts

OCCUPATION:
Secret Jedi, rebel

AFFILIATION:
Lothal rebels (prior to the Rebel Alliance)

HOMEWORLD:
Coruscant

SPECIES: Human

REALLY?!
The Inquisitor uses **THE CORPSE** of Jedi Master Luminara Unduli as **BAIT** to catch Kanan!

In numbers

100 shots
Capacity of Kanan's DL-18 blaster

14 years old
Kanan's age when the Jedi Order is destroyed

3 fights
Kanan's bar fight record for one night

2 names
Kanan Jarrus's real name is "Caleb Dume"

1.9m (6ft 3in)
Kanan's height

TOP 3

AN UNCONVENTIONAL JEDI
1. **Emotional attachments**—Kanan has feelings for Hera.
2. **Fists and blasters**—Kanan doesn't always seek peaceful solutions.
3. **Criminal contacts**—Kanan does deals with gangsters.

Kanan's favorite desserts at...
Old Jho's PIT STOP

SPACE WAFFLES AND MUJA SAUCE
Traditional favorite with fruit topping

MINCED LOTH-RAT PIE
Popular with locals

JOGAN FRUITCAKE
A crowd-pleaser from Coruscant

BLUE MILK CUSTARD
Tatooine comfort food

SPICED NYSILLIM TEA
A sweet medicinal treat

Peek behind the scenes
Kanan is voiced by actor Freddie Prinze Jr., famous for his roles in 24, Freddie, Scooby-Doo, I Know What You Did Last Summer, and She's All That.

Top 5

Kanan's jobs

1 REBEL
Leads the *Ghost* crew on Lothal with Hera Syndulla.

2 JEDI KNIGHT
Fulfills his potential as a Jedi Knight by training Ezra Bridger.

3 JEDI PADAWAN
Becomes a Jedi learner under the Old Republic.

4 FREIGHTER PILOT AND MINER
Works incognito at Moonglow on Gorse, to avoid detection.

5 BARTENDER
Helps his friend Okadiah Garson at his bar, the Asteroid Belt.

Tell me more!

SECRETS OF THE HOLOCRON
Holocrons are **storage devices** used by both **Jedi and Sith**. Only a Force-user can **open a Holocron**, activate the crystal at its core, and then project the **information** within as a **hologram**. Kanan's Holocron contains a message from **Obi-Wan Kenobi**, as well as large star maps and databases.

28

FREEDOM FIGHTER

Kanan Jarrus is a wild, quick-witted gunslinger who lives in exile near the Imperial-occupied planet of Lothal. This **wayward Jedi** helps lead the rebel crew of the starship *Ghost* in their fight against the Empire's thugs!

BEST KNOWN FOR

DESTROYING THE INQUISITOR

Kanan Jarrus

Q: What is "Form Three"?

A: When the Inquisitor confronts Kanan on the planet Stygeon Prime, he notes that Kanan favors Form Three to a "ridiculous degree." Form Three, also known as **Soresu** or the **Way of the Mynock**, is one of **seven styles** of **lightsaber combat**.

STRANGE

...BUT TRUE

Kanan has **never finished** his Jedi training. He lives **in hiding** for almost a decade, **rarely** using the **Force** or his **lightsaber**, and does his best to **avoid the Empire**.

"I lost my way for a long time, but now I have a chance to change things."
KANAN JARRUS

WHO TRAINED WHOM?

Kanan's Jedi line boasts one of the **greatest Jedi Masters**, Mace Windu, while Kanan's own Master, Depa Billaba, **sacrifices herself** to save Kanan. The rebel with a cause completes his training as a Jedi Knight by taking Ezra as a Padawan and eventually **defeating the Inquisitor**.

Master of...   Master of...

Master of...

MACE WINDU   **DEPA BILLABA**   **KANAN JARRUS**   **EZRA BRIDGER**

29

JEDI TEMPLE

Underground labyrinth • Hidden under a stone on Lothal's grasslands • Site of trials where Ezra faces his worst fears • Tests if a Padawan is ready to become a full Jedi

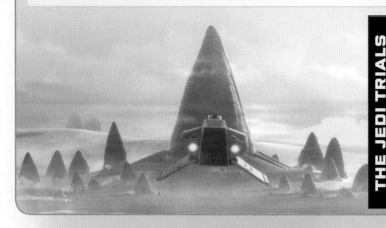

THE JEDI TRIALS

Trial 1: Teamwork Ezra must work with Kanan to open the Temple gate.

Trial 2: Isolation Ezra must leave Kanan outside and enter alone.

Trial 3: Fear Ezra confronts a terrifying vision of the Inquisitor.

Trial 4: Anger Ezra sees the Inquisitor "destroy" Kanan.

Trial 5: Betrayal Ezra has a vision of the *Ghost*'s crew saying they don't miss him.

Trial 6: Focus Ezra must stop to think about his situation, and decide to resist fear.

Trial 7: Instinct Ezra learns to trust his feelings and let the Force guide him.

Trial 8: Forgiveness Ezra realizes that revenge is not the Jedi way.

Trial 9: Protection Ezra understands that Jedi must use their power to defend others.

STREETSMART PADAWAN

Young Ezra has **grown up the hard way** on the streets of Lothal's Capital City. But after meeting the crew of the *Ghost*, he's discovered his destiny may be **greater than picking pockets**!

> "Not looking for trouble... but it sure has a way of finding me."
> **EZRA**

Ezra's fast rides

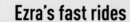

1. JUMP SPEEDER: 250KPH (155MPH)

2. 614 AvA IMPERIAL SPEEDER BIKE: 375KPH (233MPH)

3. STOLEN TIE FIGHTER: 1200KPH (745MPH)

Fast Facts

OCCUPATION: Street urchin (formerly), Jedi Padawan, rebel

SPECIES: Human

HOMEWORLD: Lothal

ACTIVITIES: Selling loot on the black market, mimicking voices, tinkering, piloting, training

FAVORITE FOODS
1. Jogan fruits
2. Meiloorun fruits
3. Any food that can be stolen from Zeb's plate

Peek behind the scenes
Ezra was the first character producer Dave Filoni sketched. He drew inspiration from the strong-willed, feisty Ralph Macchio in *The Karate Kid*!

In numbers

328 rocks
Missed by Ezra when thrown at him during lightsaber practice

150m (492ft)
Range of Ezra's slingshot

15 years old
Ezra's age

1.65m (5ft 6in)
Ezra's height

Q: Who are Ezra's parents?
A: **Ephraim** and **Mira Bridger** are two of **Lothal's first rebels**, broadcasting messages of resistance from their secret basement. Though he **doesn't know their fate**, Ezra wants to follow in their footsteps.

Top 7

Friends and enemies

1 THE REBELS
Ezra fights alongside the crew of the *Ghost* in battles against the Empire.

2 ZARE LEONIS
A buddy enrolled in Lothal's Imperial Academy, who slips information to Ezra.

3 TSEEBO
A Rodian friend of Ezra's parents and an Imperial target because of secret Empire plans that are hidden in his cybernetic head implant.

4 SUPPLYMASTER LYSTE
An officer who desperately wants to catch Ezra for stealing Imperial Academy food and technology.

5 BARON RUDOR
A famous TIE fighter pilot who has his helmet snatched by Ezra.

6 COMMANDANT ARESKO
An Imperial Academy training officer, who fails to stop Ezra from pretending to be a cadet for a secret mission.

7 THE INQUISITOR
An Imperial agent who senses Ezra's Force potential and wants to turn him into a dark side apprentice.

TOP 3

TOOLS OF THE TRADE
1. **Astromech arm**—an old R-series manipulator Ezra uses to pick electronic locks.
2. **Slingshot**—equipped with a small repulsor field that can be pulled back to shoot energy balls.
3. **Lightsaber**—constructed under Kanan's teaching, Ezra has rigged it with a blaster scope and trigger.

STRANGE

...BUT TRUE
Ezra was **born** on "Empire Day," **the same day** that the Emperor founded his Galactic Empire. All citizens must attend the parades and festivities— whether they want to or not!

Starting the Jedi path: HOW OLD IS TOO OLD?

9 YEARS OLD?
Anakin Skywalker is originally said to be **too old** to be trained as a Jedi when he is just 9 years old... look how that turned out!

14 YEARS OLD?
When Ezra starts his training he is **even older** than Anakin at 14 years, but Kanan Jarrus can see his strong Force potential.

19 YEARS OLD?
19-year-old Luke Skywalker is **much older** than Anakin or Ezra were when his Master starts to teach him the ways of the Force.

Fast Facts

HOMEWORLD:
Mandalore

ABILITIES: Languages,
computer hacking, art,
explosives, customizing
weapons and gear

AFFILIATION:
Lothal rebels

SPECIES: Human

WATCH YOUR HEAD!
From Death Watch to Sabine, the
Mandalorian helmet's classic design
remains **distinctive and menacing**.

DEATH WATCH
This warrior-cult
wears basic Mando
helmets with blue
and silver trim.

PRE VIZSLA
The leader of Death Watch
has added communications
antennae and painted his
clan crest on his helmet.

NITE OWLS
Nite Owls are a Death Watch
faction. Their helmets have a
different design, but are the
same boring blue-gray color!

SABINE
Sabine wears a
modified Nite Owl
helmet featuring her
own stylish paint job.

EDUCATING SABINE

As a student on Mandalore, Sabine
attends the Imperial Academy, where
she learns about:

 EXPLOSIVES

 WEAPONS TECHNOLOGY AND REPAIR

 COMBAT TECHNIQUES

 LANGUAGES SUCH AS AQUALISH AND HUTTESE

She later leaves the academy after
a bad experience...

**Q: What are the
creatures on
Sabine's armor?**

A: Sabine has two **animals**
painted **on her armor—**
an **anooba** on her **shoulder**,
and a **starbird** on her **chest**.
The starbird becomes the
symbol of her **rebel group**.

Peek behind the scenes
Sabine is voiced
by actress **Tiya Sircar**.
She is best known
for her roles in the
movies **17 Again** and
The Internship, and the
TV series, **The
Vampire Diaries**.

In numbers

3272 LY (Lothal Year)
The year Sabine meets Ezra
in the Lothal Calendar

250kph (155mph)
Top speed of Sabine's speeder

16 years old
Sabine's age when she helps
sabotage Empire Day

3 colors
Sabine's blaster model can fire red,
blue, and yellow plasma

1.84m (6ft)
Length of Sabine's speeder

1.7m (5ft 7in)
Sabine's height

BOMBS AWAY!

Sabine is the **weapons expert** and **resident
artist** aboard the *Ghost*. She's **smart**,
speaks **many languages**, and is always
ready to **blast** some stormtroopers!

REALLY?!
Ezra has a serious
TEENAGE CRUSH
on Sabine, but she
IGNORES his awkward
feelings toward her.

32

BEST KNOWN FOR

BLOWING UP THE EMPIRE'S STUFF

Sabine

BLASTS OF COLOR
Sabine owns a pair of **Westar-35 blasters** (nicknamed "**Jai'galaars**"), which **she has decorated** with her **own colorful designs**. This unusual artistic statement is in **stark contrast** to the **plain blasters** popular on **Mandalore**, particularly with Death Watch.

"**I want to believe we're doing good, making a difference.**"
SABINE TO HERA

Sabine decorates **Zeb and Ezra's room** with a picture of **Chopper** playing **a prank on them!**

Aqualish for beginners

"**GRUA THUN!**"
"SORRY!"

"**MOG BABB WILL WORN.**"
"I DON'T UNDERSTAND."

"**BAROO TOG NOGGRIN!**"
"I'M GLAD YOU'RE COMING!"

"**KISH TOSH KAPIK?!**"
"WHAT IS THIS?!"

"**WOOLDUG!**"
"NOW BOARDING!"

"**BUK-BUK!**"
"FINAL CALL!"

STRANGE

...BUT TRUE
Sabine's artistic and political **inspiration** comes from some unusual quarters, including **Jaynor**, a **rebel artist** on Bith and the **rebel senator Gall Trayvis**, who turns out to be a secret **Imperial agent!**

ART ATTACK
Sabine loves to give everything her **own personal touch!** She sprays her rebel graffiti on **walls**, **Imperial vehicles**, over **propaganda posters**, and even on **unconscious stormtroopers!**

33

Fast Facts

OCCUPATION: Former Honor Guard of Lasan, now a rebel on Lothal

SPECIES: Lasat

AGE: 39 dust seasons

HOMEWORLD: Lasan

ABILITIES: Bo-rifle expert, fighting stormtroopers (or in rebel-speak, "bucket-heads")

TOP 2

ZEB'S KEEPSAKES
Zeb hides mementos of his life on Lasan in his cabin on the *Ghost*.
1. **Honor Guard medallion**
2. **Tiny bag of Lasan dust**

Peek behind the scenes
Star Wars concept artist Ralph McQuarrie first came up with what became Zeb's look during his early design work for Chewbacca.

THE BIG BRUISER

If there are **bucket-heads to bash**, the rebels call on the brawniest of their bunch, Garazeb "Zeb" Orrelios. Zeb is as **strong as a Wookiee—** and **equally prickly**, especially around Chopper or that Loth-rat kid, Ezra.

How to let off steam like Zeb

"KARABAST!"
THE MOST COMMONLY USED WORD THAT EXPRESSES EXTREME FRUSTRATION

Q: Who were the Honor Guards of Lasan?

A: They were Lasan's **elite warriors**, who fell to Imperial forces when the Empire invaded the planet. Some Wookiees also received the title of Honor Guard, to **recognize their sacrifice** during the invasion.

FIGHTING INSTINCT
Stronger, swifter, and **stealthier** than humans, Lasats are **built for fighting**. Stormtroopers really **don't stand a chance**.

Zeb can **switch** between the bo-rifle's different **combat modes in just 1.36 seconds!**

BO-RIFLE HONOR
In Lasat culture, only a true Honor Guard of Lasan has the privilege to wield an AB-75 bo-rifle. With a click of a button, the weapon can change from a high-capacity blaster rifle to an electrostaff.

REALLY?!
Zeb refuses to use the Empire's **LETHAL T-7 DISRUPTORS**. He still has **NIGHTMARES** about the Imperials **DISINTEGRATING** his people **ATOM BY ATOM** with T-7s.

34

SERIOUSLY?!

Confronted by stormtroopers, Hera and Kanan pose as bounty hunters and claim that Zeb is a **RARE HAIRLESS WOOKIEE** they've captured. No one is fooled, so Zeb sorts things out with a well-placed **PUNCH**.

"There's something about the feel of their helmets on my fists."
ZEB ON STORMTROOPERS

TOP 3

BUCKET-HEAD BRAWLS

1. Smashing a stormtrooper squad at a TIE fighter platform near Lothal Capital City's marketplace.
2. Throwing troopers off their bikes when stealing supplies for Tarkintown residents.
3. Charging a group of stormtroopers that is trying to snatch a shipment of T-7 disruptors.

Peek behind the scenes
Steve Blum, Zeb's voice actor, also plays the smooth talking, snappily dressed, HoloNet News anchor Alton Kastle.

"I owe those hairy beasts. They saved some of my people."
ZEB ON WOOKIEES

STRANGE

...BUT TRUE
Zeb is **so flexible** he can squeeze his hefty 2.1m (6ft 11in) frame into the cockpit of a TIE fighter with room to spare.

WOW!...

8

The number of joints in a Lasat's toe, which helps them grapple objects with their feet

Q: Why is Zeb one of his species' few survivors?
A: Zeb's native planet, Lasan, is **invaded** by the Empire, just like the Wookiees' homeworld, Kashyyyk. Yet **instead of taking slaves** as they did with the Wookiees, the Imperials **devastate** Lasan and **exterminate** most of the Lasat.

ARCH ENEMY

Agent Kallus ordered the destruction of Zeb's homeworld, Lasan. He's the Imperial Zeb **looks forward to bashing** the most!

35

Fast Facts

AFFILIATION: Lothal's rebels

TYPE: C1-series astromech droid

MANUFACTURER: Irrelevant, seeing how often he's been patched up

PERSONALITY: Grouchy, mischievous

Control freak
Chopper has modified the *Ghost*'s systems so often, he's the **only one** who can **keep the rebel ship running**.

TOP 5

▶ **FAVORITE GADGETS**

1. **Computer probe**—connects to computers to dig out information, open doors, and control ships.
2. **Electroshock prod**—Chopper's favorite gadget, which he uses to zap both enemies and friends!
3. **Arc welder**—for repairs or cutting into objects using a tiny blowtorch.
4. **Antenna**—receives and sends data wirelessly.
5. **Grasping arms**—to pull levers, push buttons, and grab things.

BEST KNOWN FOR

PRANKING AND TEASING EZRA AND ZEB

Chopper

CRANKY MECH!

Old and grumpy, Chopper is Hera Syndulla's **faithful droid... mostly**. He's a valued member of the *Ghost*'s rebel crew, but **hates being bossed around**.

Q: What does Chopper actually do?

A: As a **C1-series astromech droid**, Chopper is the *Ghost*'s mechanic, but he can also be a real pain in the 'bot. He would **sooner play Holochess** or **pull pranks** than do his job.

In numbers

32kg (71lbs)
Chopper's weight

4 visual sensors
Including a hidden telescope

3 retractable arms
Two on his head, one on his body

2 mismatched legs
Cover plates from different droids

2-6-4
Chopper's Imperial alias

1 booster rocket
Hidden inside his body

C1-10P
Chopper's model number

STRANGE

...BUT TRUE
Chopper *really* doesn't like other astromech droids! He squabbles with R2-D2 when they meet and has been known to **push Imperial astromechs** down **sewer pipes**—or out of **starship airlocks**!

Top 5

Chopper antics

1 WISECRACKS
He always has a snarky answer or insult at the ready, but often Hera is the only one who understands him.

2 ELECTROSHOCK PRODS
He loves to zap Ezra and others with a jolt of electricity.

3 DE-BUNKING
He removes the screws from Ezra's bunk and sends him crashing down on Zeb.

4 PITCHING OVERBOARD
He helps Ezra with lightsaber training by hurling so many empty milk jugs at him that he knocks the kid off the ship!

5 FUN FIRST
He teases Zeb and Ezra rather than repair the *Phantom*, and the ship breaks down when Hera and Sabine use it later!

Peek behind the scenes

Chopper's look is inspired by the original designs for R2-D2, by legendary Star Wars concept illustrator Ralph McQuarrie.

MISSION FILE

1. **Aim:** To secretly infiltrate the Imperial Academy.
   Result: Escapes with a stolen Imperial decoder.

2. **Aim:** To ensure the *Ghost* is always mission-ready.
   Result: Plays around instead.

3. **Aim:** To hack Imperial communications tower.
   Result: Rebel message sent.

4. **Aim:** To blast the Inquisitor's TIE Advanced fighter.
   Result: Chopper is shot instead!

5. **Aim:** To go undercover to find Kanan.
   Result: Kanan's location found.

"**Waaawp waa waa warrr!**"
CHOPPER

COOL!!
Chopper is made almost entirely of many **REPLACEMENT PARTS** from **OTHER DROIDS**. Not much of him is original!

Peek behind the scenes

"If Artoo-Detoo, is your favorite dog, Chopper is the cat," says Star Wars Rebels executive producer Dave Filoni, on his approach to Chopper's personality.

TOP 3

WAYS CHOPPER GETS AROUND... AND AROUND

3 wheels—but sometimes rides along on just one, like a unicycle.
2 legs—slowly shuffles or wiggles forward... with attitude.
1 rocket booster—lets him fly, usually off the handle, for short distances.

Tell me more!

HOW TO LOSE A DROID AT SABACC

Lando Calrissian **wins Chopper** from Zeb in **Sabacc**, a popular card game. Zeb's hand totals **23** (a "**Pure Sabacc**"), but Lando holds a **2**, a **3**, and an "Idiot" card (an "**Idiot's Array**"). Lando's cards are the only combination that can beat Zeb's— and **Chopper's not happy** about it!

CHOPPER'S CRANK-O-METER
LOATHE ← → LOVE
Orders · R2-D2 · Zeb · Missions · C-3PO · Hera · Lando · Ezra · Holochess · Pranks

THE REBEL ALLIANCE

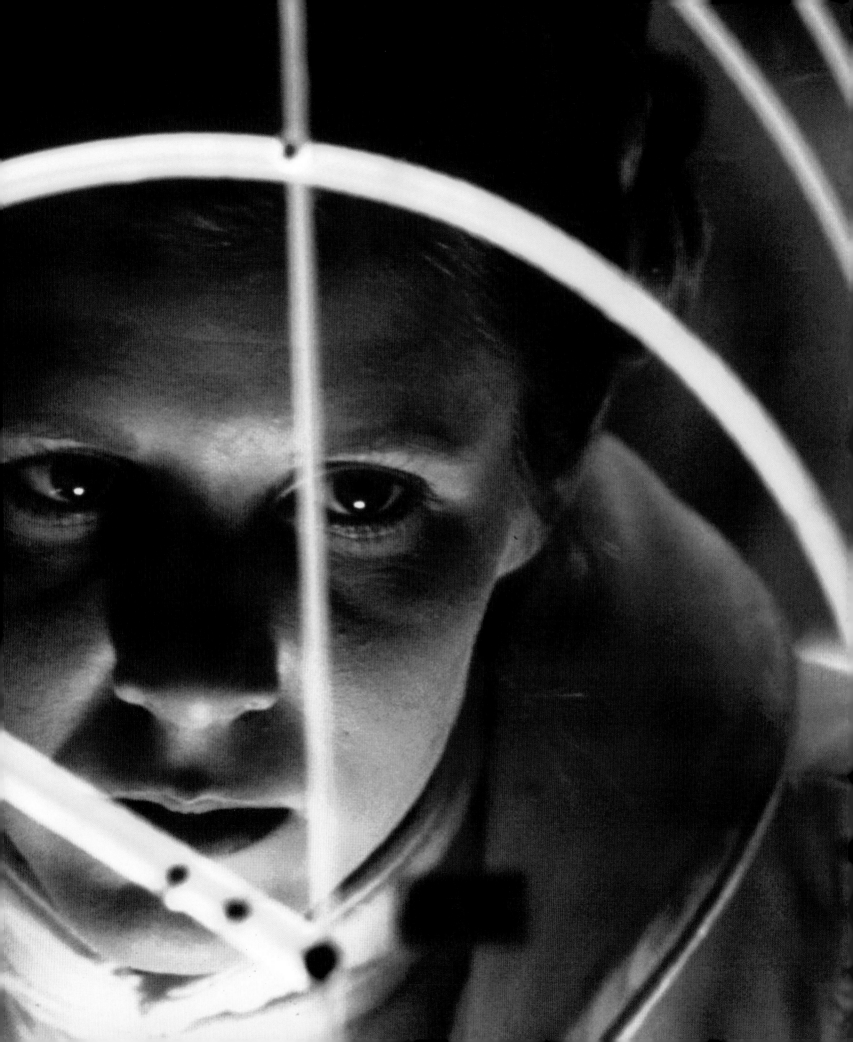

Fast Facts

OCCUPATIONS:
Moisture farmer, rebel,
Jedi Knight, Jedi Master

AFFILIATION:
Rebel Alliance

HOMEWORLD: Tatooine

ABILITIES: Piloting,
lightsaber combat,
the Force

VESSELS:
T-16 skyhopper,
T-65 X-wing fighter

1. FARM BOY
Dream big, aim **high!** Who says a farmer can't get into the Imperial Academy?

2. JEDI PADAWAN
Learn from the **very best**—Obi-Wan Kenobi and Master Yoda—and pay close attention!

3. JEDI KNIGHT
Resist the dark side, **defeat your dad, Darth Vader**, and bring balance to the Force. Easy!

4. JEDI MASTER
Save the galaxy, and be **the last Jedi standing** after the fall of the Empire.

BEST KNOWN FOR

DESTROYING THE FIRST DEATH STAR

Luke Skywalker

THE LAST JEDI

Wide-eyed and **restless,** Luke Skywalker **yearns to be a star pilot**, and dump his dull life as a moisture farmer. When he meets Obi-Wan, he learns that **his destiny lies** with something far greater—**the Force**.

STRANGE

...BUT TRUE
In their first duel, Darth Vader easily bests the **hot-headed, untested** Luke, slicing off his right hand. After barely escaping with his life, the young rebel has a **new robotic hand** fitted.

LARS HOMESTEAD

Luke's home on Tatooine •
Owen and Beru Lars's moisture farm •
Underground living quarters

"Luke's just not a farmer, Owen. He has too much of his father in him."
AUNT BERU

Blade runner
The lightsaber is an **elegant weapon** for a more civilized age. The one Obi-Wan Kenobi hands to Luke connects the farm boy with his **infamous Jedi ancestry**.

TOP 3

JEDI LESSONS FOR LUKE
1. Dueling a flying remote droid while his vision is obscured.
2. Seeing his enemy's face as his own in the Dagobah cave.
3. Dropping his lightsaber and refusing to fight his father, Darth Vader.

BATTLE ON DEVARON

The **first time** Luke ever uses his lightsaber in a duel is in a **ruined Jedi temple** on the planet Devaron. He defeats a vicious alien known as **the Scavenger**.

In numbers

2,000 credits
Sale price for Luke's speeder

1,050kph (652mph)
Speed of Luke's X-wing in atmosphere

28cm (11in)
Hilt length of Luke's second, homemade green lightsaber

19 years old
Luke's age when he leaves Tatooine

1 more season
Uncle Owen asks Luke to work on the farm before he leaves

TOP 3

FORCE-FREE FEATS
1. Swinging across the immense Death Star chasm with Princess Leia.
2. Bringing down an Imperial walker singlehandedly.
3. Defeating the ravenous rancor beast in Jabba's palace.

REALLY?!

After being savaged by a wampa, Luke is put in a bacta tank to recover. Bacta is a **CLEAR, SLIMY LIQUID** that helps the body regrow tissue, including **MUSCLES, NERVES, AND SKIN.**

WOW!...

1 in a million

The odds of Luke hitting the Death Star's exhaust port with his proton torpedoes, according to Han Solo

Peek behind the scenes
Director Richard Marquand filmed a scene in postproduction with Luke building a new, green-bladed lightsaber for *Return of the Jedi*, but the scene was cut from the final edit.

When he's not farming, young Luke relaxes by **shooting womp rats** for target practice or **racing through the treacherous Beggar's Canyon** in his T-16 skyhopper. He also hangs out with friends at Tatooine's Tosche Station, where he gets the **nickname "Wormie"!**

Q: Why does Luke leave the farm?

A: While hunting for C-3PO and R2-D2, Stormtroopers **murder** Owen and Beru Lars when they discover the droids were sold to them. With no family left, Luke accompanies Obi-Wan on his **dangerous mission to Alderaan**.

Fast Facts

OCCUPATION:
Smuggler, gambler, starship captain

AFFILIATION:
Rebel Alliance

HOMEWORLD: Corellia

VESSEL: *Millennium Falcon*

Peek behind the scenes
Han Solo was a big green alien in the original rough draft of Star Wars!

"Hokey religions and ancient weapons are no match for a good blaster at your side!"
HAN SOLO ON THE FORCE

What *is* a nerf herder?
A shepherd who tends flocks of nerfs—**smelly, scruffy, surly beasts** bred for their **thick hides**. Qualities that are **shared by their herders**, in many people's opinion.

In numbers ● ● ●

224,190 credits
The bounty that Jabba the Hutt puts on Han's head

17,000 credits
Fee for transport from Tatooine to Alderaan in the *Millennium Falcon*

1.8m (5ft 11in)
Han's height

1 DL-44 heavy blaster pistol
Han's favorite sidearm

FLY BOY

The **dashing captain** of the *Millennium Falcon*, Han Solo, has flown from one side of the galaxy to the other, usually by the seat of his pants. Solo by name, solo by nature, this **mercenary, often cocky pilot** becomes **a selfless leader of the Rebellion.**

SHOOT FIRST, THINK LATER
Han **almost blasts his friends** by shooting at a magnetically sealed door on the Death Star. It sends the **blaster bolt bouncing around the room!**

6 ways to INSULT Han!
He can **dish out the jibes**, but can he take it? Especially when they're **so close to the mark.**

SCOUNDREL!   HALF-WITTED!   SCRUFFY-LOOKING!   NERF HERDER!   SLIMY!   NO-GOOD SWINDLER!

REALLY?!
Ewoks try to **COOK HAN AS THE MAIN COURSE** at a big banquet in honor of C-3PO!

Q: What is carbonite sickness?

A: Also known as **"hibernation sickness,"** it's a **temporary condition** experienced after being thawed from carbonite freezing. Victims are briefly **left blind and very weak**, before returning to normal. Just ask Han, who is deep frozen by Darth Vader, as **a dry run** for his real target—Luke Skywalker!

TO THE RESCUE!

Just after **the Battle of Yavin**, Han and Chewie fly to the planet Cyrkon to **rescue** a member of **the Shrikes**—an elite rebel recon squadron. If the pilot, **Lt. Ematt**, fell into Imperial hands, the entire Rebellion would **be in danger**!

BEST KNOWN FOR

SAVING LUKE SKYWALKER AT THE BATTLE OF YAVIN!

Han Solo

Always the gambler, Han hangs **A PAIR OF DICE** in the viewport of the *Millennium Falcon*.

Résumé

HAN SOLO ZERO TO HERO

COCKSURE OUTLAW
On the run from Jabba the Hutt, Han Solo—smuggler, rogue, and all-around bad boy—is **only out for himself**.

REBEL HERO
Han surprises everyone, including himself, when he returns to **help the rebels blow up the Death Star**.

STRANGE

...BUT TRUE
Han, stumbling around **half blind from hibernation sickness** after being **frozen in carbonite**, accidently hits Boba Fett's jet pack, sending the bounty hunter crashing into the Sarlacc.

Never short of snarky quips—that make bad situations even worse—Han calls Jabba a "wonderful human being." No wonder the slime lord has it in for him!

PETRIFIED PRISONER
To test the freezing process, Darth Vader **encases Han in carbonite**, and gives him to Jabba as a trophy.

REBEL GENERAL
Han's skills and boldness make him a **natural rebel leader**, as he heads the successful attack on Endor.

Tell me more!

WANTED, HAN SOLO... DEAD OR ALIVE!

Han Solo is a smuggler in the pay of **crime kingpin Jabba the Hutt**. When the Empire boards Han's ship, he has to **dump Jabba's illegal cargo**. The Hutt demands that Han repay him for the loss, but when he can't, Jabba puts **a big bounty on his head!**

Q: How does a smuggler fall for a princess?

A: Han helps rescue Princess Leia in the hope of getting **a big reward**. Though he won't admit it at first, he **starts to fall in love** with her, and even becomes **jealous** that Leia is fond of Luke, not realizing until later that they are brother and sister.

43

REBEL PRINCESS

Leia Organa's **quick wits** and **bold spirit** save the day as often as they land her (and her friends) in trouble. It's very rare, but if Leia's blaster doesn't hit her targets, her **wicked one-liners** will.

Q: How does Leia know that Luke needs rescuing from Cloud City?

A: She hears Luke's call in her mind, which is an early indication that she shares Luke's sensitivity to the Force.

Fast Facts

ROLES: Princess, Imperial senator, rebel leader

AFFILIATION: Rebel Alliance

HOMEWORLD: Alderaan

ABILITIES: Strong will, sharp tongue, great shot, Force intuition

BEST KNOWN FOR

SAVING THE REBEL ALLIANCE

Leia Organa

STRANGE

...BUT TRUE
Leia braves the court of Jabba the Hutt disguised as the **bounty hunter Boushh,** with Chewie in tow as her "captive."

ON DEATH STAR II

66 From now on, YOU do as I tell you. OK? 99
LEIA, TAKING OVER HER BUNGLED RESCUE

REALLY?!

Jabba takes Leia as his new favorite slave, drooling **UNWANTED ATTENTION** all over her. But she soon **TURNS THE TABLES** on the sickening slug.

Peek behind the scenes

For Leia's hair, George Lucas was inspired by rebel hairstyles of Mexican women fighting in the Mexican War of Independence in the early 1900s.

ON ENDOR

LEIA THE LEADER

Leia isn't afraid of **leading from the front**. After the Battle of Hoth, she personally commands a perilous mission known as "**Operation Yellow Moon**." Against terrible odds, the mission is a success, sowing the seeds for the **Battle of Endor**.

GROSS!!

Leia's no **PRISSY** princess—she'll dive into stinking **GARBAGE CHUTES** that make grown Wookiees whimper!

ON HOME ONE STARSHIP

TOP 3

HEROIC MOMENTS

1. **Captured by Vader**—defies the Empire by not revealing the rebel base.
2. **Battle of Hoth**—helps lead the evacuation of Echo Base.
3. **Jabba's demise**—chokes disgusting Jabba the Hutt with her slave chains.

You know you're a great rebel when you...

- **Hide the Death Star plans** in R2-D2 so they safely reach the rebel forces.
- **Assist** Generals Dodonna and Rieekan at the **Battles of Yavin and Hoth.**
- Help **destroy Death Star II's shield generator** to seal the fate of the Empire.

ON CLOUD CITY

Tell me more!

FORCE-FUL FAMILY

When Luke abandons his Jedi training to **rescue his friends**, Obi-Wan's spirit sighs, "that boy is our last hope." But Yoda replies, "there is another," referring to Luke's twin sister, Leia. She is also **strong with the Force,** even though she doesn't yet realize it.

Love interest...

Han Solo may have won Leia's heart... but that doesn't mean he can let down his guard!

In numbers

50,000 credits
Leia's asking price for Chewie, from Jabba the Hutt

2187
Leia's Death Star detention cell number

100 shots
In Leia's small sporting blaster pistol

19 years old
Leia's age when she's captured by Darth Vader

1.5m (4ft 11in)
Leia's height

Fast Facts

HOMEWORLD: Kashyyyk

DIET: Wild plants, berries, meat, spices—the hotter, the better!

AFFILIATION: Allies of the Republic and the Rebel Alliance

DISTINGUISHING FEATURE: Shaggy, water-shedding coat of hair

Peek behind the scenes
Chewbacca's voice was created by sound designer Ben Burtt. He used animal noises from walruses, dogs, and lions, but mostly from a bear named Pooh!

TEMPER TANTRUMS
Peace-loving Wookiees are aggressive **only when provoked**. But watch out—they have **ferocious tempers**.

FURRY FIGHTERS

Wookiees are big, strong, hairy creatures, but **don't** call them dumb—they're highly **intelligent** and easily take offense. Wookiee hero Chewbacca (aka Chewie) is Han Solo's **copilot**, a **loyal rebel**, and a **fine example** of his species.

"ALWAYS THINKING WITH YOUR STOMACH"
Chewie's big appetite lands the rebels in trouble on Endor. When he finds a **tasty dead critter** hanging in the forest, he tugs on it and **triggers** an Ewok **trap**!

Peek behind the scenes
Chewbacca as a copilot was inspired by George Lucas's own dog, Indiana, who used to sit in the passenger seat of his car.

Tarfful's long-gun cost a big **2,000** credits to make!

WOOKIEE GADGETS

Wookiees are expert craftsmen who blend modern technology like **blasters** and **lightsabers** with traditional materials such as **wood, precious stones, and metals**.

Chewie's bowcaster **breaks tradition** with its automatic cocking system.

Q: Why does Chewie get mad when Luke tries to handcuff him?

A: It **reminds** him of his time as a **slave** of the Empire, which **imprisons and enslaves many Wookiees**. Chewie was **rescued** by Han Solo, and **pledged a Wookiee life debt** to him in thanks.

46

WOW!...

400

The average lifespan of a Wookiee in years

HOW TO INSULT CHEWIE!

The kind-hearted Chewbacca puts up with a lot of name calling—even from his friends.

"Flea-bitten furball!"
C-3PO, as Chewie repairs him

"Big furry oaf!"
Han Solo, as the two of them climb into the Death Star's trash compactor

"Walking carpet!"
Leia, minutes after they first meet

"Hairy beast!"
C-3PO strikes again!

"THING!"
An unpleasant Imperial officer, who soon regrets his outburst

Spice Mine slaves

Wookiee Wullffwarro and his son Kitwarr are sent to **work as slaves** in the Kessel Spice Mines. Spice is **valuable** not only for its medicinal uses, but also as **an illegal drug**.

In numbers

150kg (331lb)
Average weight of a male Wookiee

100kg (220lb)
Average weight of a female Wookiee

19 ammo cases
In Chewbacca's bandolier

12 years old
Age that male Wookiees undergo initiation rituals to enter adulthood

7 dreadlocks
Hang from chieftain Tarfful's head when he fights in the Clone Wars

3 Wookiee languages
Shyriiwook, Thykarann, Xaczik

OUCH!!
Chewie is a **SORE LOSER**—he's been known to **RIP** opponents' arms out of their **SOCKETS** if he doesn't win a game!

How to speak Shyriiwook

"WYAAAAAA!"
"HELLO!"

"ROOOARRGH UR ROO."
"I HAVE A BAD FEELING ABOUT THIS."

"RRRRUGH ARAH-AH-WOOF?"
"HOW DO YOU TAKE YOUR COFFEE?"

"WWWAH RRROOOAAAH WHA?"
"WANT TO PLAY HOLOCHESS?"

"AARRR WGH GGWAAAH!"
"JUMP TO HYPERSPACE!"

STRANGE

...BUT TRUE

Wookiees can't speak Basic because of their **strange vocal chords**—but they can understand it. **Barking, growling, moaning, and roaring** are typical features of the Wookiees' many different dialects.

AWESOME!!
C-3PO was once **MISTAKEN FOR A GOD** by the primitive Ewoks on the moon of Endor!

In numbers

75kg (165lbs)
C-3PO's fully assembled weight

21+ bits and bobs
On R2-D2 including arms, scanners, and accessories

15 opening panels
On R2-D2's head

10 known masters
Of C-3PO

1.09m (3ft 6in)
R2-D2's height

DOUBLE TROUBLE!

Protocol droid C-3PO and his astromech ally R2-D2 are **an unlikely pair**. Although C-3PO dislikes excitement, he often follows R2-D2 on **thrilling exploits across the galaxy**.

Peek behind the scenes
Sound designer Ben Burtt created R2-D2's voice, in part, by recording himself making baby noises on a synthesizer!

Q: What is R2's secret mission to Tatooine?
A: Princess Leia gives R2 the **stolen plans** to the Empire's **Death Star** battle station. He must deliver them safely to Obi-Wan Kenobi to **save the galaxy**.

"We're doomed!"
C-3PO TO R2-D2

STRANGE

...BUT TRUE
C-3PO is **blasted to bits** by Imperials on Cloud City. When Chewbacca reassembles him, the Wookiee places **C-3PO's head on backward**!

WOW!...

6,000,000+

Forms of communication known to C-3PO

Fast Facts

MANUFACTURER:
R2-D2: Industrial Automaton
C-3PO: Cybot Galactica

MAKE:
R2-D2: R-series Astromech droid
C-3PO: Protocol droid

PRIMARY FUNCTIONS:
R2-D2: Navigation, repair
C-3PO: Etiquette, protocol, translation

DROID-IN-CHARGE:
R2-D2 (although **C-3PO** thinks it is him!)

Q: **Why is R2-D2 so hard to understand?**

A: R2 talks in **binary**, a language of **beeps** and **whistles**. C-3PO often has to **translate** to help everyone else understand what he's saying.

Peek behind the scenes
Actor Anthony Daniels **couldn't sit down** while wearing the C-3PO costume for the first film, and had to **lean against a board** between his scenes.

BEST KNOWN FOR

SAVING QUEEN AMIDALA'S ROYAL STARSHIP

R2-D2

TOP 5

ASTROMECH ACCESSORIES
1. **Lightsaber launcher**—for top secret missions.
2. **Electro magnetic power charge arm**—also handy for zapping Ewoks.
3. **Rocket boosters**—for flying through the air.
4. **Buzzsaw**—to cut through almost anything.
5. **Drink dispenser**—to serve guests at parties.

R2-D2 accidentally **electrocutes himself** trying to plug into a **power outlet** on Cloud City! He thought it was a computer terminal.

What *is* R2-D2 saying?

"SPRRPFT!"
"PHOOEY!"

"WRRK-WRRK. WEEEEEOOP!"
"I SAID *COUNTER*CLOCKWISE!"

"WAH-WAH. WRRY-WRRY-NAHWIKOO!"
"LET'S GET OUTTA HERE!"

"PRRP-PAREE-PAREE PAIRREEOOP?"
"WHAT COULD POSSIBLY GO WRONG?"

HOW TO MAINTAIN YOUR DROID

C-3PO can always be **patched up** with spare parts or **upgraded** to be better than new. Just make sure you keep a screwdriver, a large can of oil, and spray paint handy—not to mention **a bucketload of compliments**.

How does **Darth Vader** use the **Force** to **throw objects** at his foes?

BAD GUYS, BOUNTY HUNTERS, AND THE UNDERWORLD

Where does **Jabba the Hutt** keep the **delicious frogs** he loves to **snack on?**

What makes **Darth Sidious's face melt** during his **battle** with Mace Windu?

50

CHAPTER 2

THE SITH

Fast Facts

OCCUPATION: Politician and Sith Lord in hiding

HOMEWORLD: Naboo

ABILITIES: Force lightning, lightsaber dueling, keeping big secrets

> "Your feeble skills are no match for the power of the dark side…"
> **DARTH SIDIOUS**

THAT FIGURES!!
Darth Sidious **ELIMINATES** his **OWN SITH MASTER,** Darth Plagueis, after learning everything he knows.

END OF AN ERA
The Emperor's reign comes **crashing down** when Darth Vader **hurls him down an energy shaft** on the second Death Star! Vader's dying efforts save his son, Luke, whom the evil Emperor was about to slay.

Q: What is a Sith?

A: The Sith are the **ancient enemies** of the **Jedi**. Long ago, a group of **Jedi fell to the dark side**, becoming the **first Sith**. Ever since, they have tried to **destroy the Jedi** and **rule the galaxy**.

Top 5

Reasons to rule the galaxy

1 **ABSOLUTE POWER!**
No one will question your authority.

2 **APPLAUSE**
The Senate will cheer your every move.

3 **EFFICIENCY**
People work harder when they know you're watching.

4 **THE BEST HEADQUARTERS**
Your office on the Death Star comes with a great view!

5 **THE THRONE**
The Emperor deserves the best chair in the galaxy.

In numbers

23 years
As Galactic Emperor

3 Sith apprentices
Trained by Darth Sidious

2 red-bladed lightsabers
Wielded with devastating skill and power

1.73m (5ft 8in)
Palpatine's height

Q: Does Darth Sidious share his power with other Sith?

A: Never! Sidious **shares power with no one**. When **Darth Maul** and his brother **Savage Opress** become **rivals** to his power, Sidious **defeats them both**.

54

PURE EVIL

Obsessed, devious, and absolutely ruthless, this scheming Sith Lord has been known by many titles—Senator from Naboo, Supreme Chancellor, and finally Emperor. His true identity is Darth Sidious, and ultimate power is his only goal.

BEST KNOWN FOR

RULING THE GALAXY WITH AN IRON FIST!

Palpatine

STRANGE

...BUT TRUE

Darth Sidious **rarely leaves his palace** and often appears via **hologram**. He prefers to let his **minions** do the **dirty work**!

Peek behind the scenes

It took four hours to apply the makeup and prosthetics to transform actor Ian McDiarmid into the Emperor!

Tell me more!

MASTER MANIPULATOR

Palpatine works for years **to bring down the Jedi and the Republic**. He secretly creates the **crisis on Naboo** to **become Chancellor** and then becomes **both leader of the Republic** and **secret leader of the Separatists** during the **Clone Wars**. With the galaxy in chaos, he uses the clones to **wipe out the Jedi** and takes **full control** of, well, everything.

DON'T MESS WITH THE DARK SIDE!

During a fight with Mace Windu, Palpatine **fires Force lightning** at his opponent, who reflects the dark energy back at the Sith, revealing his true, evil nature. Palpatine's **face melts** and his **eyes, nails, and teeth turn a sickly yellow**. After he becomes Emperor, he hides his disfigured appearance in Imperial propaganda broadcasts.

PALPATINE'S RISE TO POWER

EMPEROR...
With the Jedi destroyed and in full control of the Senate, Palpatine becomes Emperor.

CHANCELLOR...
During the Naboo crisis, Palpatine is elected Chancellor of the Republic.

SENATOR...
Sheev Palpatine represents the planet Naboo in the Galactic Senate.

BLOOD BROTHERS

Darth Maul and Savage Opress are brothers, but they are bound together by more than just family ties. Born into the **Nightbrothers**—a terrifying warrior clan—they inherit the same fierce desire to wreak revenge on their enemies, no matter the cost.

BEST KNOWN FOR

SLAYING FAMOUS JEDI MASTER QUI-GON JINN

Darth Maul

Darth Maul lives for years on the JUNK PLANET Lotho Minor. It is almost entirely COVERED in trash, DUMPED there from other worlds!

Top 3

Items in Maul's hunting kit

1 PROBE DROID
Tiny "dark eye" can infiltrate small places Maul could never go.

2 ELECTROBINOCULARS
Night vision and magnified zoom locate distant targets.

3 SITH INFILTRATOR
Maul's personal starfighter is equipped with high-tech stealth systems.

Opress **DESTROYS** his other **BROTHER**, Feral, to prove his **LOYALTY** to the Nightsisters!

"At last we will have revenge."
DARTH MAUL

DARTH MAUL'S GUIDE TO LOOKING EVIL

- A dark, hooded cloak is a great way to carry out your Master's evil work in secret and frighten your foes into the bargain.
- Lost your legs? Try scouring Lotho Minor's junkyards! An injured Maul finds himself six articulated-like legs after his own are chopped off by Obi-Wan.
- Ask your sisters for help. Maul acquires a new set of cybernetic legs from the Nightsisters, to renew his vendetta against Obi-Wan.

DATHOMIR

Homeworld of Nightbrothers and Nightsisters • Planet bathed in blood-red sunlight • Place where Nightsisters use dark magic to enlarge and transform Opress into a vicious monster

Fast Facts

AFFILIATION: Sith Lords, Nightbrothers

SPECIES: Dathomirian Zabrak

ABILITIES: Strong with the dark side of the Force. Both are skilled with double-bladed lightsabers, while Opress also wields an enchanted pike

Young Opress is raised in an ISOLATED Nightbrother village on Dathomir, where women and outsiders RARELY visit.

Peek behind the scenes
Writer Katie Lucas used Frankenstein's monster as inspiration when writing the vengeful character of Savage Opress.

"Brother, let us share our strength."
SAVAGE OPRESS

REALLY?!
Opress and Maul's **MOTHER** gave them their first **TATTOOS** before their **FIRST BIRTHDAY!**

STRANGE ...BUT TRUE
Nightsister Asajj Ventress tests **six Nightbrothers** in brutal combat. The last warrior standing, Savage Opress, impresses Asajj enough to become her apprentice.

In numbers

26.5m (86ft 11in)
Length of Maul's Sith Infiltrator

12 years
Period of time Maul is believed to be dead after his battle with Obi-Wan

9 horns
Crown Opress's head

2.18m (7ft 2in)
Opress's height after Mother Talzin's shaman spell increases his size from 1.89m (6ft 2in)!

Q: How does Maul survive being cut in half?

A: The power of **anger**! Maul draws on his Master's dark side lessons to harness his **rage** and **stay alive** after Obi-Wan **maims** him in a duel on Naboo! **Rumor** has it that his top half fell down a reactor shaft into a **trash container**, which was then shipped to Lotho Minor.

 Tell me more!

HEADHUNTED BY WITCHES

Nightbrothers like Savage Opress are raised as **servants** of the **witches who rule Dathomir—the Nightsisters**. The **strongest** Nightbrother warriors are **tested and selected** from their clans, to receive the power of the Nightsisters' dark side **magic** and to become their **mates**.

57

DOOKU'S PALACE

Headquarters of the wealthy House of Dooku • Located above a cliff on Serenno • Main tower is 119m (390ft) tall

BEST KNOWN FOR

LEADING THE SEPARATIST ALLIANCE

Count Dooku

"Welcome to Serenno. You have been invited here because you are the best bounty hunters in the galaxy."

COUNT DOOKU, AT "THE BOX" TOURNAMENT

TURNING TRAITOR

Dooku completes his fall from the light side when he **eliminates his friend, Jedi Sifo-Dyas**, under orders from Darth Sidious. With Sifo-Dyas gone, the **Sith take control of the Jedi's clone army.**

 ## Tell me more!

TAUGHT BY THE BEST

As a Jedi, Dooku is **trained by Master Yoda**, who considers him the Order's **greatest student—** and its **greatest failure**. In turn, Dooku takes Qui-Gon Jinn as his first and most famous Padawan.

THE GREAT BETRAYER

The **despicable Count Dooku** battles the Republic with his **massive droid armies**. The Jedi are in a desperate race to stop him before he **conquers the galaxy!**

In numbers

80 years old
Dooku's age when he duels Yoda on Geonosis

40 seconds
Length of lightsaber duel with Yoda

13 bounty hunters
Assembled for "The Box" tournament

7 radiator grooves
In Dooku's Sith lightsaber

2 lightsabers
1 as a Padawan, 1 as both Jedi Knight and Sith

1.93m (6ft 4in)
Dooku's height

Peek behind the scenes

George Lucas had a very different villain in mind for Attack of the Clones. But when Christopher Lee joined the cast, Count Dooku was specifically created for the legendary actor to play!

JOURNEY INTO DARKNESS

One of the **most brilliant Jedi Knights**, Dooku yearns for greater power and **leaves the Order** to lead the **Separatist army** as Count Dooku. He later **embraces the dark side as Darth Tyranus**, disciple to evil Sith Lord Darth Sidious.

Fast Facts

ROLE: Sith apprentice to Darth Sidious

ALIASES: Count Dooku, Darth Tyranus

HOMEWORLD: Serenno

SPECIES: Human

FASHION TO DIE FOR

Count Dooku **loves wearing fine clothes!** His **elegant cloak** is woven by famous tailors on the distant planet Vjun, and is a symbol of the Counts of Serenno. His boots are made of **rare rancor leather,** as is his belt, which holds his **stylish yet deadly red crystal lightsaber.**

"**I've become more powerful than any Jedi. Even you.**"
DOOKU TO YODA

Q: Who are the "Lost Twenty"?

A: Count Dooku is the **20th Jedi Master to quit the Order** over differences with his fellow knights. There are **memorial statue busts** of each of these former Jedi displayed at the **temple on Coruscant**.

TOP 5

DOOKU'S COMBAT STYLE
1. Slashes his victims with a lightsaber.
2. Chokes the life from his opponents.
3. Zaps his rivals with Force lightning.
4. Force-smashes his enemies against a wall.
5. Runs away when all else fails.

REALLY?!
Dooku **CUTS OFF ANAKIN'S HAND** in the Battle of Geonosis. The young Jedi later gets his revenge in a duel with Dooku on General Grievous's flagship: **DOOKU LOSES BOTH HANDS— AND HIS HEAD!**

WOW!...

1,000,000
Hondo Ohnaka's asking price in credits for selling Dooku to the Republic

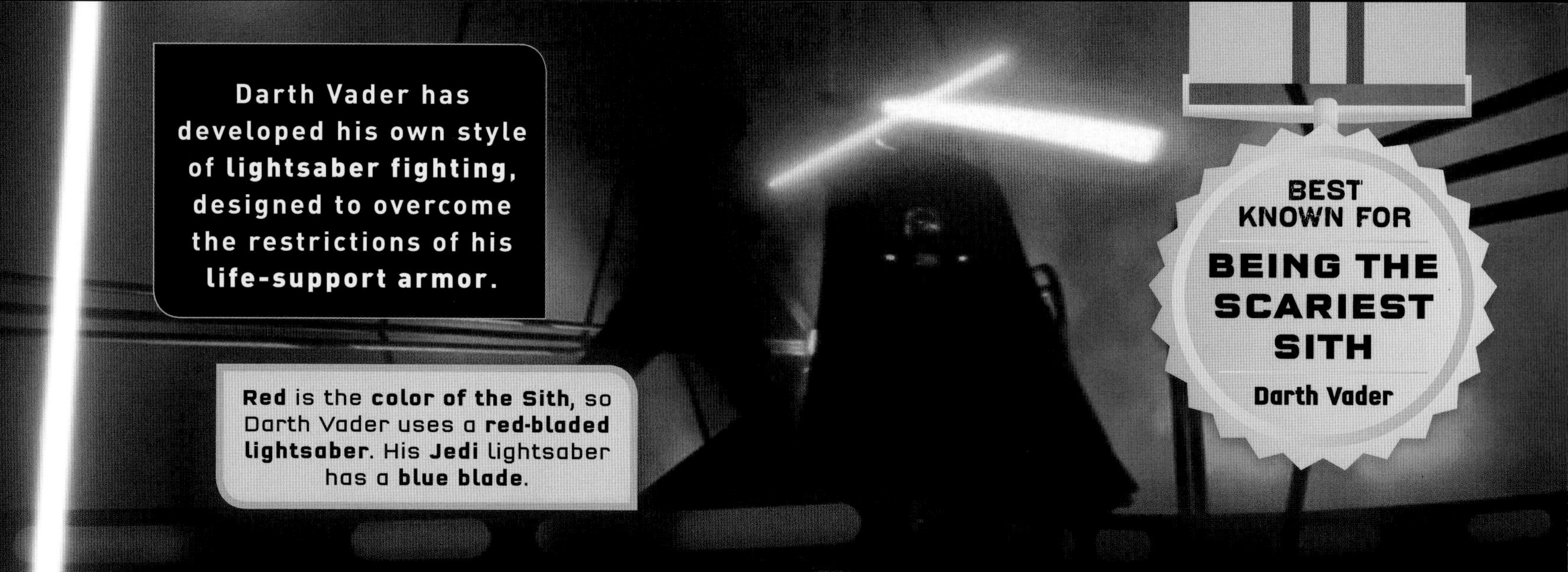

Darth Vader has developed his own style of **lightsaber fighting**, designed to overcome the restrictions of his life-support armor.

Red is the **color of the Sith**, so Darth Vader uses a **red-bladed lightsaber**. His **Jedi** lightsaber has a **blue blade**.

BEST KNOWN FOR

BEING THE SCARIEST SITH

Darth Vader

THE FALLEN ONE

Darth Vader is **feared greatly** as the Emperor's Sith apprentice. He was once the noble Jedi Knight Anakin Skywalker, but the **dark side** and horrific injuries have transformed him into a terrifying cyborg.

REALLY?!
Darth Vader often wins arguments by **FORCE CHOKING** people who disagree with him.

Darth Vader's **menacing growl** is artificially created because his **damaged vocal cords** make his natural voice very weak.

TOP 5

WAYS DARTH VADER DEFEATS HIS ENEMIES
1. Outfights them with his lightsaber.
2. Outflies them in his personal TIE fighter.
3. Hurls objects at them with Force telekinesis.
4. Picks them up and throws them around with Force levitation.
5. Force chokes them.

Peek behind the scenes
Darth Vader's face mask and helmet were inspired in part by the headdress worn by Japanese Samurai.

60

Fast Facts

HOMEWORLD: Tatooine (as Anakin Skywalker)

AFFILIATION: Galactic Empire

SITH MASTER: Darth Sidious

SPECIES: Cyborg (previously human)

CHILDREN: Luke Skywalker, Princess Leia Organa

SUBORDINATES: The Inquisitor, 501st Legion

Embracing the **DARK SIDE** makes your **EYES** change color! Anakin Skywalker has blue eyes, but they **TURN YELLOW** when he becomes Darth Vader.

"Join me, Luke, and together we can rule the galaxy as father and son.**"**
VADER TO LUKE SKYWALKER

Q: Who turns Anakin to the dark side?

A: Darth Sidious takes advantage of **Anakin** when he is at his most vulnerable. Devastated by a **vision of his wife Padmé dying**, the young Jedi agrees to become Sidious's apprentice after the Sith Lord promises him that only the powers of the **dark side can save her**. Once on the path to evil, there's **no turning back** for Anakin.

You know you're sliding to the dark side when you...

1. **Wipe out** the Tusken Raiders who kidnap your mother.
2. **Execute** Count Dooku after defeating him in battle.
3. **Destroy** younglings at the Jedi Temple.
4. **Massacre** Separatist leaders on Mustafar.
5. **Force choke** your beloved wife, Padmé.

FAN FACT

Darth Vader's **breathing sound** was made by breathing through **scuba gear**.

STRANGE ...BUT TRUE

Darth Vader **cannot eat normally** because he has been **injured so badly**. Instead, his life-support armor **feeds nutrient fluids** directly **into his body**. In his private chamber, Vader can **remove his helmet** and use a **feeding tube**.

Q: How does Vader try to lure Luke to the dark side?

A: Vader pleads with Luke to **help him defeat** his evil Sith Master, **Emperor Palpatine (Darth Sidious)**, so that they can **rule the galaxy together** as father and son.

In numbers

120kg (265lbs)
Darth Vader's weight in his armor

10 protective layers
In Vader's armor

4 artificial limbs
Worn by Vader

2.03m (6ft 8in)
Vader's height in his armor

2 lightsabers
Owned by Vader

THE SEPARATISTS

Fast Facts

NAME: Trade Federation

LEADER: Viceroy Nute Gunray

MEMBERS: Mostly Neimoidians

AFFILIATION: Wherever there's profit to be made

AIM: Control all galactic trade routes, ports, and freighters

PROTECTED BY: Huge army of battle droids

REALLY?! Neimoidians are big **SHOWOFFS**! They dress in the latest fashions and wear the most expensive and bizarre robes and hats, no matter how **SILLY** they look.

BEST KNOWN FOR

COWARDICE AND ROLLING IN MONEY

Trade Federation

"**Is she dead yet? I am not signing your treaty until I have her head on my desk!**"

GUNRAY TO THE SEPARATISTS ON SENATOR AMIDALA

Tell me more!

THE SWINDLERS ARE SWINDLED

The Trade Federation are **duped** by scheming Palpatine (Darth Sidious), when he **goads** them into **blockading** the planet Naboo with their army of battle droid ships. It's all part of Palpatine's **secret plan** to **increase** his political powers and ignite a **galactic war**!

GREEDY GRUBS

The **powerful, corrupt Trade Federation** runs most of the galaxy's shipping routes. It will do anything to increase profit and avoid paying the Republic's taxes. Who leads it? Step forward grasping **Nute Gunray** and his **Neimoidian cronies**!

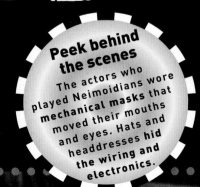

Peek behind the scenes
The actors who played Neimoidians wore mechanical masks that moved their mouths and eyes. Hats and headdresses hid the wiring and electronics.

64

STRANGE

ONCE A GRUB...
Gunray was born a **"grub,"** a **maggot-like larva** that grows into a walking, talking, cheating Neimoidian.

...BUT TRUE
For the first **seven** years of their life, Neimoidian larvae are forced to **compete** with each other over a limited food supply. Only those who learn to be **greedy** and **hoard the most food survive**—it's great practice for a life of **swindling**!

Battle droids—the gears of war
The Trade Federation prefers to rely on **battle droids** to save its skin, rather than hiring warriors for its security forces. Why? Battle droids are **cheap, disposable, easily mass-produced**, and will fight **without demanding payment**! What's more, the Federation has a business deal with the Geonosians to build **countless battle droids** in their huge **factories**, in preparation for war.

Q: Who are the Separatists?
A: Led by Count Dooku, this **influential movement** is made up of different groups of people **who want to leave** the Republic. One of those groups is the wealthy Trade Federation, who **secretly provide** the Separatists with battle droids, which become **soldiers** of the **mighty Separatist army**.

Who helps Nute Gunray in his dodgy trade deals with alien species?
This delightful job belongs to silver protocol droid **TC-14**, Gunray's **personal assistant**. Her memory banks are **wiped regularly** to stop her from developing a personality... or a conscience.

FEDERATION FLAGSHIP
Named *Saak'ak* • *Lucrehulk*-class freighter • 3,170m diameter (10,400ft) • Quad turbolaser cannons • Cloaking device • Orbits Naboo during the blockade and invasion

REALLY?!
In return for supporting the Separatists, Gunray **DEMANDS** that Count Dooku **SLAYS** Gunray's longtime nemesis, Senator Padmé Amidala of Naboo!

WOW!...

139,000

The number of battle droids that just one Trade Federation battleship can carry

STRANGE

...BUT TRUE
Nute Gunray **never** puts his own neck on the line. Why would he, when he can **trick** others into doing his **dirty work**? It's the Neimoidian way of doing business!

65

Fast Facts

OCCUPATION:
Kaleesh warlord
turned Supreme
Commander of
the droid army

AFFILIATION:
Separatists

HOMEWORLD:
Kalee

Kalee

Peek behind the scenes
Sound designer Matthew Wood supplied the voice of General Grievous in Revenge of the Sith and Star Wars: The Clone Wars.

CYBORG FIEND

General Grievous is the **maniacal cyborg Commander** of the Separatist droid army. Most of his body has been **mechanically enhanced**, making him a match for even the strongest Jedi. But *never* **call him a droid**!

LUNAR HIDEOUT

Castle on the third moon of Vassek • Full medical facilities • Spare part storage • Defended by MagnaGuards

"This is the lair of General Grievous!"
KIT FISTO REALIZING HE HAS BEEN LURED INTO A TRAP

Tell me more!

NEW, IMPROVED GRIEVOUS
General Grievous **chooses** to **upgrade his organic body** with synthetic parts. But with his **heart and lungs failing,** he has serious breathing problems and a **nasty cough!**

Q: Who maintains Grievous's mechanical parts?

A: Droid **A4-D** is Grievous's personal medical droid. **Part doctor, part mechanic,** he repeatedly repairs the cyborg's body after battles with the Republic.

66

BEST KNOWN FOR

KEEPING THE LIGHTSABERS OF DEFEATED JEDI

Grievous

WOW!...

95%

The amount of Grievous's body parts that are mechanical

STRANGE

...BUT TRUE
Grievous will **knock the heads off** his own battle droids when they **make him mad**—which is **most of the time!**

Grievous's **FACE MASK** must be painfully **PEELED FROM HIS FACE** with a fusion cutter when it needs to be replaced.

"More machine than alive... though more dangerous for it."
YODA ON GRIEVOUS

"I do not care about your politics… (or) your Republic. I only live to see you die!"
GENERAL GRIEVOUS TO THE JEDI COUNCIL

AWESOME!!
Grievous can **WALK ON SIX LIMBS** like a crab when he needs to move quickly.

SPEED DEMON
General Grievous's **personal ground transport** is a modified **Tsmeu-6 personal wheel bike**. It is **swift and powerful**—strong enough to **crush soldiers in its path**.

REWIRED!

Even **bits of Grievous's brain** have been **cybernetically rebuilt** to make him a smarter, faster fighter.

Height chart

Giant General
In his **cyborg body**, Grievous **towers over** his frequent foe, **Obi-Wan Kenobi**.

2m	
1.5m	
1m	
0.5m	

Grievous
2.16m (7ft 1in)

MagnaGuard
1.95m (6ft 5in)

Obi-Wan Kenobi
1.82m (6ft)

Battle droid
1.91m (6ft 3in)

DEADLY WITCH

Asajj Ventress is a **lethal Nightsister witch** with a dangerously close connection to the **dark side of the Force**. Betrayed more than once by those she trusted, Ventress has learned that she can only **rely on one person: herself**.

REALLY?!
Ahsoka Tano nicknames her sworn enemy, Ventress, a **HAIRLESS HARPY, BOG WITCH, and LOWLIFE.**

TOP 3
ASSASSIN SKILLS
1. **Stealth**—expertly ambushing unsuspecting enemies.
2. **Martial arts**—superior hand-to-hand combat with much larger foes.
3. **Force choke**—capable of lifting enemies by the neck, using only the Force.

Tell me more!

SISTERHOOD OF DARKNESS

The Nightsisters are a mysterious **sect of warrior witches** who tap into **ancient dark Force magicks** to help them **deceive enemies**. Ventress learns a great deal from their mystical leader, **Mother Talzin** (below center).

Résumé: Asajj Ventress

- **Student assassin**
  Trains as Sith Lord Count Dooku's apprentice throughout much of the Clone Wars.

- **Nightsister**
  Betrayed by Dooku, Ventress returns to Dathomir to fight alongside her witch sisters.

- **Bounty hunter**
  Works for herself as a bounty hunter after the Nightsisters are destroyed.

MISSION ACCOMPLISHED

"I don't fear you, Jedi."
VENTRESS TO YODA

STRANGE

...BUT TRUE
Ventress is known to **kiss** her foes before **finishing them** with her lightsaber!

NO WAY!!
Ventress is strong enough with the dark side of the Force to **FORCE CHOKE MANY FOES AT ONCE!**

Top 4

Dangerous missions

1 KIDNAPPING THE HUTT
Ventress takes Jabba's son, Rotta, hostage and pins the crime on the Jedi.

2 NEIMOIDIAN RESCUE
The assassin must save Separatist leader Nute Gunray from the Jedi, or silence him before he spills secrets!

3 ATTACK ON KAMINO
Ventress tries to steal the original Jango Fett DNA from the Republic... and nearly succeeds!

4 JOINING FORCES WITH THE JEDI
Ventress teams up with Obi-Wan Kenobi to defeat the Nightbrothers Darth Maul and Savage Opress, who terrorize the galaxy.

Q: Is Ventress a Sith?

A: Ventress draws her power from the **dark side** of the Force and is mentored by Count Dooku, yet she is **not fully trained in the ways of the Sith**. Her skills are **undisciplined** and not perfect.

Peek behind the scenes
The name Asajj was inspired by the character "Asaji" in the 1957 samurai film *Throne of Blood* by Akira Kurosawa, one of George Lucas's favorite directors.

Ventress **TATTOOS HER HEAD, FACE, AND MOUTH** after embracing the **DARK SIDE.**

TEST OF FURY
Not one to take the easy way out, Ventress faces off against **six Nightbrother clan leaders** in the Test of Fury, a **trial she must pass** to **become a full assassin**!

Flirting with danger
Ventress **eliminates the bounty hunter Oked** when he tries to **flirt with her** at Mos Eisley Cantina!

Ventress's bounty hunter armor icon is a **snake.** She chose it because, like her, snakes are **misunderstood** creatures: They are thought to be evil even when they are not.

A CLOSER LOOK

69

THE EMPIRE

Fast Facts

AFFILIATION: Galactic Empire (some are former Republic officers)

OBJECTIVE: To maintain the Empire's grip on the galaxy and crush any rebellion

CLAIMS TO FAME: Carrying out terrorism, destroying planets, enslaving people, torturing suspects

SPECIES: Almost always human

"Fear will keep the local systems in line. Fear of this battle station!"
GRAND MOFF TARKIN ON THE FIRST DEATH STAR

Q: What is the Tarkin Doctrine?
A: Tarkin convinces the Emperor that the best way to govern the Empire is **through fear**. Just the threat of unleashing **unimaginable destructive power** on any rebellious star system is enough to make its inhabitants toe the line. This leads to the development of the **dreaded Death Star**.

Death Star

Peek behind the scenes
Peter Cushing, who played Grand Moff Tarkin, often wore slippers during filming, because the boots for his Grand Moff costume hurt his feet. He was usually filmed above the waist only!

COMMAND AND CONTROL

Who does Emperor Palpatine rely on to mercilessly enforce his **oppressive rule** across the galaxy? **Imperial military officers!** Their position gives them authority over most stormtroopers, and many senior officers hold **tremendous power in their hands.**

Tell me more!

EMPIRE POSTER BOY

And the award for the Empire's **most talented military officer** goes to... Tarkin. Titled both Grand Moff and Governor, his career spans **naval service** in the Galactic Republic, a planetary **governorship**, and control of the **Death Star project**. Strategic skills and a love for scaring everybody into good behavior make Tarkin **one to watch.**

72

REALLY?!
Imperial officers live in **DREAD OF FAILURE.** Darth Vader Force chokes **ANYONE WHO MAKES A MISTAKE!**

TOP BRASS ON THE FIRST DEATH STAR

GRAND MOFF WILHUFF TARKIN
Governor of the Outer Rim Territories, Death Star Commander.

ADMIRAL ANTONIO MOTTI
Chief of the Imperial Navy, member of the Joint Chiefs.

GENERAL CASSIO TAGGE
Chief of the Imperial Army, member of the Joint Chiefs.

ADMIRAL WULFF YULAREN
Deputy Director, Imperial Security Bureau and Naval Intelligence Agency.

FASHION TO DIE FOR
Designed by Tarkin himself, Imperial officers' uniforms are **functional, not fancy**. Different colors indicate the branches of service—olive-gray for **Navy and Army**, black for **stormtrooper officers**, and white for **Intelligence**. No decorations or medals are worn—they would clutter the uniforms' **clean lines**.

TOP 4
IMPERIAL OFFICER TRAITS
1. Ruthlessness
2. Ambition
3. Intelligence and resourcefulness (occasionally)
4. Loyalty to the Emperor (especially when it's in their best interest)

IMPERIAL RANK GUIDE

You can tell an Imperial officer's rank by looking at the **plaques they wear on the left side** of their uniforms. Status is indicated by **red, blue, or yellow** plastic squares in rows that are attached to metal plates.

GRAND MOFF:

ADMIRAL:

CAPTAIN:

WOW!...

2,000,000,000
Lives lost when Alderaan is destroyed in mere seconds by the Death Star, on Tarkin's order

73

Fast Facts

BEST KNOWN FOR

MUTTON-CHOP SIDEBURNS

Agent Kallus

SECRET SERVICE

Ruthless Agent Kallus is one of the Imperial Security Bureau's **best spies** at tracking down the Empire's enemies. However, a group of the **rebel scum** on Lothal continues to escape him!

Q: Who sets up the ISB?

A: **Cunning Palpatine** founds the ISB, a secret police organization, when he declares himself Emperor. It is dedicated to **rooting out enemies** of the New Order.

ISB CENTRAL OFFICE

Located on Coruscant • Huge building complex spans several city blocks • Houses personnel and equipment to analyze intelligence data

How to speak in ISB spy slang

"AUDITING"
WHEN SUSPECTS KNOW THEY'RE BEING INVESTIGATED

"CRUSTBUSTING"
PROVOKING A SUSPECT TO COMMIT A CRIME

"SCATTERING"
INTERROGATING A SUPPOSED INNOCENT IN HOPES THEY REACT SUSPICIOUSLY

"JABBA"
FRAMING A WANTED SUSPECT FOR A CRIME TO MAKE SURE THEY ARE ARRESTED

WANTED: HAVE YOU SEEN THESE CRIMINALS?

GALL TRAYVIS
Exiled Senator—hacks the HoloNet News with broadcasts, to accuse the Empire of crimes.

CHAM SYNDULLA
Twi'lek Resistance leader and icon—forges group to fight Imperial occupation.

TSEEBO
Worker at the Imperial Information Office—disappears with top secret Empire plans.

"FULCRUM"
Mysterious figure operating under codename—connected to many rebel cells.

OBI-WAN KENOBI
Jedi General of the Clone Wars—rumored dead, could be in contact with surviving Jedi.

74

"Next time they move, we'll be waiting for them—to snuff out that spark before it catches fire."
KALLUS ON THE LOTHAL REBELS

Q: **How many ISB agents does it take to change a lightbulb?**

A: **Two.** One to remove it, another to accuse the first of **disloyalty**!
(A common joke among Imperial Intelligence agents)

021
Kallus's ISB code number

REALLY?! Kallus once defeated a Lasat Honor Guard in a duel and took the warrior's bo-rifle as a **TROPHY**—a **HUGE INSULT** to Lasats!

Top 6 ISB branches

SURVEILLANCE—analyzes data for POTENTIAL THREATS.

INTERROGATION—claims to have a 95 PERCENT SUCCESS RATE in discovering useful data from questioned suspects.

RE-EDUCATION—BRAINWASHES suspects to support the Empire.

ENFORCEMENT—special operations units act as BACKUP for field agents.

INVESTIGATION—uses data to SUPPRESS rebel activity.

INTERNAL AFFAIRS—searches for TRAITORS within the Imperial ranks.

Tell me more!

HOW TO LEAD A CRACKDOWN
Agent Kallus orders the use of T-7 disruptors—**deadly weapons banned** under the Republic—to decimate the planet-wide resistance on Lasan and **silence the Lasats** once and for all.

Did you know it's taken just 14 years for the ISB to grow from a handful of agents to a vast network double the size of Imperial Intelligence?!

Top 5

Powers of high-ranking ISB agents like Kallus

1 **COMMANDING** stormtrooper squads.

2 **OVERRIDING ORDERS** of civilian and military authorities.

3 **NOT FOLLOWING** standard Imperial rules.

4 **REPLACING SUSPICIOUS** military officers.

5 **TAKING CONTROL** of military vehicles and vessels, even Star Destroyers, if necessary.

TOP 4

REASONS KALLUS IS THE CREAM OF THE CROP

1. Graduates head of his class.
2. Crushes major and minor threats to the Empire all over the galaxy.
3. Refuses promotion many times to remain on the front line.
4. Wipes out the rebellion on Lasan.

Top 5

You know you're a Pau'an if...

1 YOUR HOME IS A HOLE
Pau'ans dwell in darkness.

2 YOU LIKE YOUR MEAT RAW
Hold the veggies! Pau'ans only eat raw, bloody meat.

3 YOUR EARS ARE SENSITIVE
Pau'ans have hypersensitive hearing and wear coverings to protect their ears.

4 YOU'RE PALE AND WRINKLY
Pau'ans have pasty skin with deep, vertical grooves.

5 YOUR TEETH ARE POINTY
That raw meat diet develops razor-sharp teeth!

"I admire your persistence. Ready to die?"
THE INQUISITOR TO EZRA

WHO ANSWERS TO WHOM?

The Inquisitor is an agent of Darth Vader. His special mission gives him unique privileges to command others.

DARTH SIDIOUS/ EMPEROR PALPATINE
The supreme power

STORMTROOPERS
Obey all higher ranks without question

GOVERNOR TARKIN AND DARTH VADER
Ruthlessly enforce the Emperor's orders

IMPERIAL OFFICERS
Strictly comply with the Inquisitor's orders

THE INQUISITOR
Can commandeer required Imperial forces while on missions, aside from Governor Tarkin

WOW!...

10.6

The time it takes the Inquisitor to identify a Jedi's fighting style, in seconds

Fast Facts

OCCUPATION: Imperial Inquisitor

AFFILIATION: The Empire

HOMEWORLD: Utapau

SPECIES: Pau'an

Q: Is the Inquisitor a Sith?

A: No! Darth Sidious can have only one apprentice at a time, and currently that is Darth Vader. The Inquisitor is merely **a trained servant** and **assassin**, although he does possess **limited dark side Force powers**.

The Inquisitor is in the Jedi Archives. What could he find there?

- **Historical records** dating back thousands of years
- **Maps** of the entire galaxy
- **Scientific, mathematical,** and **astronomical journals**
- **Engineering** and **technology documents**
- **Jedi records** of the Sith

- **Details** of **geography** and **cultures** of the galaxy
- **Knowledge** about **zoology** and **botany** of the galaxy
- **Secrets about** how the Jedi use **the Force**
- **Biographies** of Jedi and their **identification details**

TOP 3

INQUISITOR'S LIGHTSABER MODES
1. **Single blade**—default mode with crescent handle.
2. **Double blade**—extended mode with disk handle.
3. **Spinning**—automated mode with rotating handle.

Q: What is the Inquisitor's evil mission?

A: Darth Vader has given the Inquisitor a **cruel mission**—one that the cold-hearted Pau'an pursues with **grim efficiency**. He must hunt down the Jedi and **turn their young apprentices to the dark side—or slay them!**

Tell me more!

MIND OVER LIGHTSABER
The Inquisitor is proud of his **intelligence** as well as his skill with his infamous **red lightsaber**. He uses logic to **assess a Jedi's abilities**, discover the **combat forms** they favor, and even work out **who their mentor is**. Yet even the Inquisitor is **not invincible!**

HE'S BEHIND YOU!
The Inquisitor's special ship can **fire tracking beacons onto fleeing rebel ships!** His TIE Advanced v1 prototype is **superior** to normal TIE fighters, due to his super-secret missions.

REALLY?!
Even Imperials are not safe from the Inquisitor. He is under orders to **EXECUTE** officers Grint and Aresko as **PUNISHMENT** for their failures.

LIGHTSABER COMBAT FORMS
The **Jedi Order** recognizes **seven forms of lightsaber combat**. The **Inquisitor** has learned to **use**—and **counter**—all of them!

Form I: Shii-Cho
The oldest, rawest form, often used when all else fails.

Form II: Makashi
Specialist form for duels with Sith opponents.

Form III: Soresu
A defensive form, for fighting in tight quarters.

Form IV: Ataru
An acrobatic form, best suited for open spaces.

Form V: Shien / Djem So
Focuses on turning attacks back on opponents.

Form VI: Niman
Combines double-bladed lightsaber combat with other Force abilities, like pushes and lifts.

Form VII: Juyo / Vaapad
The most aggressive and unpredictable form.

JEDI HUNTER

Lean, mean, and **clad in high-necked armor,** the Inquisitor cuts a **sinister figure**. This loyal servant of the Empire will not rest until the last Jedi—or future Jedi—are **terminated**.

Peek behind the scenes
The Inquisitor is voiced by British actor Jason Isaacs, famous for his role as Lucius Malfoy in the *Harry Potter* movies.

TOP 3

CLASHES WITH KANAN JARRUS
1. **Stygeon Prime**—Kanan and Ezra outrun the Inquisitor.
2. **Fort Anaxes Base**—Ezra saves Kanan by using the Force to command a fyrnock to attack the Inquisitor.
3. **Tarkin's Star Destroyer**—Kanan eliminates the Inquisitor.

BUCKET-HEADS

Faceless in their iconic white helmets, **stormtroopers** are the **soldiers** of the Imperial military. Their **total loyalty** to the Empire and **boldness in battle** make them **feared** throughout the galaxy.

Q: Why are stormtroopers such lousy shots?

A: They're not! And don't let them hear you say that! Despite their **bulky armor**, stormtroopers are **excellent shots**. It's just that the galaxy's heroes are very **tricky targets**—especially those that use the Force!

Fast Facts

LEADER: Stormtrooper commander

AFFILIATION: The Empire

AKA: Bucket-heads (rebel nickname)

ENERGY SETTINGS
1. Sting 2. Stun 3. Lethal force

BlasTech E-11 blaster rifle
The stormtroopers' standard issue weapon is based on the clone troopers' DC-15a blaster.

WOW!...

25,984

Stormtroopers are assigned to the Death Star!

STRANGE

...BUT TRUE
Despite what some people think, stormtroopers are **not clones**. They are **trained civilians**. Underneath their armor, they all look **very different**.

THE BIG GUNS
Some stormtroopers get training to use specialized weapons, including heavy blasters, close-combat weapons, and even flamethrowers!

IF THE HEADGEAR FITS

WEAR IT!!!

Tell me more!

YOUR EMPIRE NEEDS YOU
The Empire doesn't enlist stormtroopers. Instead, it uses **propaganda** to attract recruits. **Posters** showing stormtroopers as brave peacekeepers have inspired **millions of volunteers** to sign up for training.

78

BEST KNOWN FOR

RUTHLESSLY ENFORCING THE LAWS OF THE EMPIRE

Stormtroopers

The stun setting on blasters can knock a target unconscious.

Stormtrooper cadets who struggle in training are given the **most unpleasant jobs** to do around the Academy.

The stormtrooper helmet's plastoid shell protects its wearer from both physical and energy attacks.

In numbers

2,500+ stormtroopers
Can be carried on an Imperial Star Destroyer

501st Battalion
Darth Vader's personal battalion

19 years
Before the Battle of Yavin, the Stormtroopers Corps is founded

0 stormtroopers
The number who have turned traitor (according to Imperial records)

The first rebels poke fun at **stormtroopers** and their **chunky helmets** by calling them **"bucket-heads."** Some people have **no respect!**

REALLY?!
Stormtroopers don't use their own **NAMES**. They are known only by **IDENTIFICATION NUMBERS**.

Talk like a trooper

STORMTROOPERS OFTEN LET THEIR BLASTERS DO THE TALKING. WHEN THEY DO SPEAK, THEY GET STRAIGHT TO THE POINT.

"BLAST 'EM!"

"FREEZE. DON'T MOVE!"

"SET FOR STUN!"

"STOP THAT SHIP!"

"ALL RIGHT MEN, LOAD YOUR WEAPONS!"

Peek behind the scenes
Concept artist Ralph McQuarrie's **earliest illustrations** for Star Wars showed stormtroopers carrying lightsabers!

IMPERIAL ACADEMY

Grueling training for stormtrooper cadets • Headed by Commandant Aresko and Taskmaster Grint • Located in Capital City on Lothal

"By the time you complete your training, you will be ready to serve your Emperor."
COMMANDANT ARESKO

PHASE I CLONE TROOPER
Basic plastoid body shell is used by early clone troopers. Cheap, but uncomfortable.

PHASE II CLONE TROOPER
More advanced armor used during later stages of the Clone Wars. Easily adaptable.

STORMTROOPER
All-purpose shock trooper gear replaces clone trooper armor when Empire is founded.

TROOPERS THROUGH TIME

These warriors in white armor have been marching across the galaxy for decades. Their armor has become a symbol of their ruthlessness, and they have worn many different kinds over the years. Whatever they're wearing, it's best to steer well clear—where stormtroopers go, bad things tend to happen!

SCOUT TROOPER
Light armor allows greater mobility for scouting missions and riding speeder bikes.

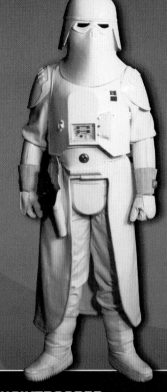

Peek behind the scenes
When Luke says "I can't see a thing in this helmet!" while disguised as a stormtrooper, it was actually an ad-lib by Mark Hamill, due to the helmet prop not having proper eyeholes!

SANDTROOPER
Modified stormtrooper armor keeps wearer cool under desert suns.

SNOWTROOPER
Insulated thermal armor and helmet keeps body warm in cold conditions.

FIRST ORDER FLAMETROOPER
Specialized armor used by First Order flame units. Helmet is designed to reduce glare.

FIRST ORDER STORMTROOPER
Updated, more versatile armor design used by rank and file stormtroopers of the First Order.

BOUNTY HUNTERS

Fast Facts

FATHER: Jango Fett

SON: Boba Fett

OCCUPATIONS: Bounty hunters

AFFILIATION: Highest bidder

AIM: To earn a good living by catching people with a price on their heads

Jango Fett

REALLY?! Boba shares the **GENETIC PATTERN** of his father, making him Jango's **TWIN** as well as his **ADOPTED SON!**

Boba Fett

FAMILY BUSINESS

For **two** generations, the name Fett **has struck sheer terror** into the hearts of wanted men. Few can escape capture from the **scarily skilled bounty hunters** Jango and Boba Fett.

HOW TO CLIMB THE CAREER LADDER BY JANGO

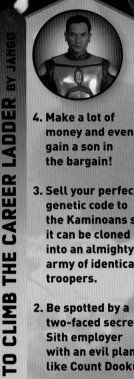

4. Make a lot of money and even gain a son in the bargain!

3. Sell your perfect genetic code to the Kaminoans so it can be cloned into an almighty army of identical troopers.

2. Be spotted by a two-faced secret Sith employer with an evil plan, like Count Dooku.

1. Build a reputation as one of the most ruthless warriors in the galaxy.

WHO TRAINED WHOM?

From an early age, Boba is taught how to fight by his father, who also supervises the flash-training of new clone troopers. After Jango comes to a grisly end, Boba learns more about bounty hunting from the assassin Aurra Sing.

JANGO FETT

AURRA SING

CLONE TROOPERS

BOBA FETT

DON'T FORGET!
Nobody knows how he came into possession of it, but Jango **wears the armor** of the legendary **Mandalorian** warriors. Boba **patches together** his own suit in **memory** of his father.

Peek behind the scenes
Concept artist Joe Johnson designed Boba's armor to look like Boba had **cobbled together** pieces taken from wanted men that he'd **captured or destroyed.**

84

BEST KNOWN FOR

DELIVERING HAN SOLO TO JABBA THE HUTT

Boba Fett

Boba **blows up** his father's **Mandalorian helmet**! He rigs it with a bomb to lure Mace into a trap.

TOP 3

TARGETS PURSUED BY BOBA

1. **Mace Windu**—sliced off Jango's head with his lightsaber. Boba swears revenge!
2. **Wookiees**—a captured Wookiee is a big boost to a bounty hunter's status.
3. **Han Solo**—the most famous catch of all, wanted in every star system...

WOW!...

20,000,000

Credits paid by Kaminoans for Jango's genetic code

Q: What's that loop Boba is wearing around his shoulder?

A: Some say it's **hair** from an **unlucky Wookiee**, but others say the **braid** of a Jedi **Padawan**! No one dares ask...

"**He's no good to me dead!**"

BOBA TO VADER ON HAN SOLO BEING TESTED FOR CARBONITE FREEZING

In numbers

200,000 clone soldiers
Of Jango produced in the first batch for the Republic!

70m (230ft)
Maximum vertical height of Jango's Z-6 jetpack thrusters

10 years old
Age that Boba is orphaned

1 blaster shot
All it takes for Jango to take out a giant reek beast in the arena

Special heirloom
Boba **inherits** Slave I, Jango's customized Firespray-class interceptor of the kind made to **guard prison moon** Oovo 4. If it's **good enough** to foil desperate criminals, then it's **good enough** for Jango!

Top 3

Special weapons in Jango's arsenal

1 WRIST WHIPCORD THROWER
Shoots out cord to tangle up his opponent and stop them from moving.

2 MISSILE LAUNCHER
Explosive missile on both jetpack models Jango owns.

3 ZX MINIATURE FLAME PROJECTOR
Casts a 5m (16ft 5in) cone of ferocious fire from gauntlet.

HIRED GUN

Mad, bad, and **dangerous to know,** Cad Bane has been considered the **best bounty hunter in the business** ever since Jango Fett met a sticky end. **Loyal to the highest bidder,** he never lets morals get in his way.

BEST KNOWN FOR

WEARING HIS COOL WIDE-BRIMMED HAT

Cad Bane

TOP 3

BANE'S EMPLOYERS

1. **Darth Sidious**—Bane only ever deals with Darth Sidious's hologram form.
2. **The Hutts**—he regularly works for the bosses of these crime families, especially Jabba.
3. **Count Dooku**—Bane is hired by Dooku after successfully competing in "The Box."

STRANGE...

...BUT TRUE

Bane takes part in Count Dooku's competition on Serenno, in which **13 bounty hunters** enter a **deadly, maze-like device called "The Box."** Bane is one of the five bounty hunters who escape alive, and are then hired to **eliminate Chancellor Palpatine.**

REALLY?!

No job is too ghastly for Bane... he even **KIDNAPS CHILDREN** who may become future Jedi!

REPUBLIC JUDICIARY DETENTION CENTER

A prison on Coruscant • Inmates include Bane, Ziro the Hutt, Boba Fett, and Bossk • Bane breaks out with Rako Hardeen (Obi-Wan) and Moralo Eval

In numbers

1,000,000 credits
The price Separatists will pay Bane for one dead Jedi

75kg (165lbs)
Weight

51 years old
Equivalent age in human years

3x normal rate
Amount Bane is paid to steal a Jedi Holocron for Sidious

1.85m (6ft 1in)
Height

Peek behind the scenes

Bane's sidekick, Todo 360, is voiced by Seth Green, best known for his work on Buffy the Vampire Slayer and Robot Chicken.

"Not the first time I've broken out of this stink hole."

CAD BANE TO MORALO EVAL AND RAKO HARDEEN (OBI-WAN IN DISGUISE)

86

"I'm your worst nightmare, pal!"
CAD BANE

Fast Facts

OCCUPATION:
Bounty hunter

HOMEWORLD:
Duro

SPECIES:
Duros

SPECIALTIES: Armed combat, maintaining a large network of bounty hunter contacts

HOW TO OUTFLY THE LAW

Bane is given a *Rogue*-class starfighter called *Xanadu Blood* by Darth Sidious, which he flies during several missions. Built by the Baktoid Armor Workshop, the ship is upgraded with **a cloaking device** and **superior weapons**.

NO WAY!! **TODO 360** is Bane's very loyal service droid. So guess who he uses as a **BOMB** during the Senate **HOSTAGE CRISIS?**

WOW!...

2,500,000

The Republic's reward for Bane's capture, in credits

Top 6

Assignments

1 HOLOCRON HEIST
Bane sneaks into the Jedi Temple Archives to steal a Holocron.

2 CHILDREN OF THE FORCE
Bane kidnaps Force-sensitive children for Darth Sidious.

3 SENATE PLANS
Bane takes R2-D2 and C-3PO captive to steal their data about the Senate.

4 SENATE HOSTAGE CRISIS
Using the Senate as a diversion, Bane breaks Ziro the Hutt out of prison.

5 HUNT FOR ZIRO
Bane is hired to recover Ziro once again.

6 CRISIS ON NABOO
Bane tries to assassinate Chancellor Palpatine.

87

THE UNDERWORLD

Fast Facts

HOMEWORLD: Most Hutts are from Nal Hutta

LEADERS: Jabba and The Hutt Grand Council

AFFILIATION: Gangsters and crime families

CLAIM TO FAME: Hutts are selfish, disloyal, and devious gluttons— and those are their good points!

"Your mind powers will not work on me, boy."
JABBA TO LUKE SKYWALKER

How to speak Huttese

"CHUBA!"
"HEY YOU!"

"PATEESA"
"FRIEND"

"MOULEE-RAH"
"MONEY"

"BOSKA!"
"LET'S GO!"

"MEE JEWZ KU!"
"GOODBYE!"

TOP 3

YUCKY THINGS HUTTS EAT

1. **Gorgs**—large amphibians that are sold in Mos Espa Market for the princely sum of seven wupiupi.
2. **Slime pods**—organisms bloated with gas that float in the swamps on Nal Hutta.
3. **Klatooine paddy frogs**—Jabba keeps an aquarium of fresh and tangy frogs by his throne at all times.

Top 5

Horrible Hutt Council members

1 JABBA DESILIJIC TIURE
A gambler and slaver who rules the council via hologram and through his representative, Gardulla Besadii the Elder.

2 GORGA DESILIJIC AARRPO
The council's **dishonest, dapper accountant**, who likes wearing a monocle with his fancy headgear.

3 AROK THE HUTT
Always-angry council member who **threatens to eliminate** Jabba's uncle, Ziro.

4 ORUBA THE HUTT
Ancient albino who **pampers himself** with fine clothing.

5 MARLO THE HUTT
A **deceitful dealer** in the slave markets of Zygerria.

Q: How do the Hutts pay for stolen goods?
A: With wupiupi, a type of **currency** used by the Hutts on Tatooine. **16** golden wupiupi coins equal **one** trugut, **four** truguts equal **one** peggat, and **one** peggat can get you around **40** Republic credits. So save your wupiupi!

REALLY?!
Hutts can't grow hair so some **WEAR** a small creature called a **SHA'RELLIAN TOOP** instead!

WOW!...

1,358

Jabba's weight in kg (2,994lbs)

90

SLIME LORDS

The **drooling, ruling** Hutts are a **slug-like** species who control the **criminal underworld** in the Outer Rim. These crooks avoid the wars of the Republic and the Empire—they only look out for themselves, and none more so than the **infamous Jabba!**

GRUESOME HUTT FATES

1. **Ziro** (Jabba's uncle)—shot twice by his love Sy Snootles on Teth, under orders from Jabba.
2. **Oruba**—sliced by Savage Opress's lightsaber on Nal Hutta.
3. **Jabba**—strangled by Leia Organa on Tatooine.

FAN FACT

The **slimy** sound of Jabba the Hutt was mainly made using a bowl of **melted cheese.**

Tell me more!

SLIMY DOUBLE-CROSSING, NO-GOOD SWINDLERS

The Hutt crime gangs make money from illegal activities. Some buy and sell **slaves**, while others **smuggle goods**, or **gamble on podracing** and **gladiator matches**. Then there are those who lend money and charge **too much** interest. And if that's not bad enough, some Hutts even **hire pirates**!

TOP 3

HUTTS WITH TATTOOS

1. **Jabba**—the Desilijic crime family's tattoo is carved on his right arm.
2. **Arok**—his "kajidic" (crime gang) symbol is tattooed on his upper left arm.
3. **Ziro**—covered in bright tattoos indicating his connection to the Hutt world Sleheyron.

In numbers

35,000 credits
The reward Jabba pays bounty hunter Boushh for capturing and bringing Chewbacca to his palace

604 years old
Jabba's age at his death

23 Sha'rellian toops
Stacked high on the head of Ziro's Mama!

15% interest
Charged by Jabba on the debt Han Solo owes him, after Han dumps the Hutt's illegal cargo from his ship

3.7m (12.1ft)
Gardulla's length, from head to tail

Hutts start out as **tiny Huttlets** like Rotta, at just 0.43m (1ft 5in) in height. With great age they reach **legendary sizes**, like Ziro's Mama at 4.52m (14ft 10in)!

HUTT GRAND COUNCIL

Ruled by the heads of the five Hutt crime families • Council Hall located on Nal Hutta, surrounded by murky swamps • Place for meetings and parties

Mandalore's moon, Concordia, is dotted
with **disused mines**. Deep inside, the
Death Watch wait, their minds fixed
on the **violent glories of the past**.

Peek behind the scenes
At first George Lucas had concept artists Ralph McQuarrie and Joe Johnston create a **supertrooper** for The Empire Strikes Back, which later became **Boba Fett**. This would later **inspire** the Death Watch.

“ **We are the Death Watch,
descendants of the warrior faith
all Mandalorians once knew.** ”
PRE VIZSLA

SHADOW ARMY

Conniving Concordia Governor **Pre Vizsla
pretends to support** Mandalore's peace-loving
Duchess Satine Kryze. Secretly, he **leads her
greatest foes**—the **Death Watch warriors**.

STRANGE...

...BUT TRUE
As leader of the Death Watch,
Pre Vizsla wields the **deadly
Darksaber**—an **ancient,
black-bladed** lightsaber that
Mandalorians of his clan
stole from the Jedi Temple
millennia ago.

REALLY?!

Death Watch member
BO-KATAN KRYZE is the
Duchess's sister, so
TALKING POLITICS
over family dinners is
probably unwise!

Tell me more!

GIVE PEACE A CHANCE?
Mandalorians were once **feared
mercenaries** and **bounty hunters**.
They even fought the Jedi—and **often
won**. But constant war **ravaged the
planet** and now Duchess Satine
Kryze and her New Mandalorians
want to **embrace peace**. However,
not everyone agrees with them!

92

BEST KNOWN FOR

REVIVING MANDALORE'S WARRIOR TRADITION

Death Watch

How to speak Mando'a

"AKAANIR"
"FIGHT"

"NAAK"
"PEACE"

"NAASTAR"
"DESTROY"

"BESKAR'GAM"
"ARMOR"

"NARUDAR"
"YOUR ENEMY'S ENEMY"

"KYR'TSAD"
"DEATH WATCH"

In numbers

4,000,000
Population of Mandalore

412,000
Population of Concordia

5,000 warriors
Rumored to be in the Death Watch

17.97m (58ft 11in)
Length of a Mandalorian shuttle

4 crew members
Needed to man the Death Watch
Kom'rk-class fighter *Gauntlet*

OUCH!!
The Death Watch **CAPTURES** Obi-Wan Kenobi on Concordia and tries to **SMASH** him in a **ROCK GRINDER!**

MANDALORE

Centuries of war have turned much of planet into desert • Citizens live in bio-cube cities • Capital Sundari City is home to Duchess and Ruling Council • Death Watch hide out in Mandalore's moon, Concordia

Mandalorian armor looks cool!

That's because it *is* cool! Mandalorian armor is packed with the latest must-have gadgets, such as **missile-launching jetpacks, armed gauntlets, magnetized boots,** and **helmets with tactical displays**. What's not to like?

Q: What's that symbol on Pre Vizsla's helmet?

A: It's the image of a **Mandalorian shriek-hawk** (or "jai'galaar") diving at its prey. The ancient symbol of Clan Vizsla, it is also used as the **insignia of the Death Watch**.

"Mandalore's violent past is behind us. Our warriors moved to Concordia. They died out years ago."

DUCHESS SATINE TO OBI-WAN KENOBI

93

Fast Facts

OCCUPATION: Pirates

AFFILIATION: Neutral

WEAPONS: Blaster pistol, electrostaff, sharp wits

SPECIES: Weequay

Peek behind the scenes
Flying saucers from 1950s' science-fiction stories inspired the design of Hondo's pirate ships!

Q: What is Hondo's favorite ship?

A: Hondo's pride and joy is his **Personal Luxury Yacht 3000**. It's named *Fortune and Glory*—after his favorite things!

MEET THE PIRATE GANG!

Hondo employs a gang of Weequay pirates. They're reliable as fighters, but as friends—watch your back!

TURK FALSO
Resents taking orders from Hondo. If he sees a chance to betray his boss, he'll grab it!

GWARM
Lieutenant in the pirate gang and a real bully. Dreaded by farmers all over Felucia.

PARSEL
Copilot on Hondo's ship. Good pilot. Bad buddy. His loyalties are always up for sale.

JIRO
Pirate lieutenant. Betrayed Hondo by joining Darth Maul. Then betrayed Maul.

PIIT
One of the few female pirates on Florrum. Noted for her purple-painted peg leg!

R5-P8
Not your regular astromech. He has a pirate blaster mounted on the top of his head.

PIRATE MENACE

STRANGE

...BUT TRUE
Tough, **leathery skin** helps Weequay to endure the **harsh conditions** on their desert planet **Sriluur**.

A **shrewd pirate** and **kidnapper**, Hondo Ohnaka leads a gang of **greedy bandits** on the Outer Rim planet of Florrum. He's chasing **fortune and glory**—in that order!

Top 4

Most profitable missions

1 KYBER CRYSTAL THEFT
Pirates will even steal from Jedi. They find that younglings make the easiest victims.

2 ARMS DEALING
Selling weapons to mercenaries pays big. Who cares what they're used for?

3 STEALING CROPS
Local farmers can't defend themselves. Tough!

4 HOSTAGE TAKING
Important hostages mean big paydays, so aim high!

MOTHER KNOWS BEST
Hondo's mom **sold him** when he was a boy, but luckily she taught him all about **hostage-taking** first! In Hondo's words: "As my sweet mother always said, 'Son, if one hostage is good, two are better, and three, well, that's just **good business!**'"

NO WAY!!
Pirates often blow their entire haul of **ILL-GOTTEN GAINS** on **DRINKS AND EATS** at Hondo's bar.

MARAUDING MOTHERSHIP
Hondo commands his gang from a *Corona*-class armed frigate. **No one** in the Outer Rim has **escaped their daring raids!**

AWESOME!!
Weequay can be **GOOD GUYS**, too! Que-Mars Redath-Gom was a **JEDI KNIGHT** who fought for the Republic in the Battle of Geonosis.

94

Q: Whose side are the pirates on?

A: Hondo and his pirates wish to remain **neutral** during the Clone Wars. They may **briefly take sides** if their lives (or particularly fat profits) are at stake, but their **loyalty is always short-lived**.

BEST KNOWN FOR

ABDUCTING COUNT DOOKU AND STEALING HIS LIGHTSABER!

Hondo Ohnaka

HONDO'S PIRATE BASE

Marketplace for illegal trading • Full of listening devices and traps for hostages • Fleet of WLO-5 battle tanks • Fully stocked bar • Situated on Florrum

"**I smell profit. Nice, fat, juicy profits!**"
HONDO

REALLY?! **FISTFIGHTS** often break out at Hondo's **PIRATE BASE**, usually over nothing at all!

"But you know what I always say: Speak softly, and drive a big tank."
HONDO

STRANGE

...BUT TRUE
Pirates enjoy **betting** on **Mukmuk fights**—battles between Hondo's two Kowakian **monkey-lizards**.

Tell me more!

FRIENDS AND FRENEMIES
Hondo rubs shoulders with some of the most **infamous people** in the galaxy. He was a longtime **buddy of Jango Fett,** and bounty hunter **Aurra Sing is his ex-girlfriend.** Hondo often runs into **Jedi heroes** such as **Obi-Wan Kenobi, Anakin Skywalker,** and **Ahsoka Tano.** When he does, he will either **befriend or betray** them—whichever is most profitable!

In numbers

200 passengers
Capacity of a pirate frigate

6 parsecs
Distance between Florrum and the desert planet Vanqor

1.89m (6ft 2in)
Average height of a Weequay pirate

0.47m (18.5in)
Length of a typical pirate's peg leg

TOP 3

PIRATE VEHICLES
1. *Flarestar*-class attack shuttle
2. Pirate speeder tank
3. Starhawk speeder bike

Almost everything Hondo owns is **stolen,** including his **snazzy red jacket!**

Who narrowly stops the **Ewoks** from **feasting** on the rebels **for dinner?**

WEIRD AND WONDERFUL BEINGS

Where do **rogues, smugglers,** and **alien misfits** settle their **debts** on Tatooine?

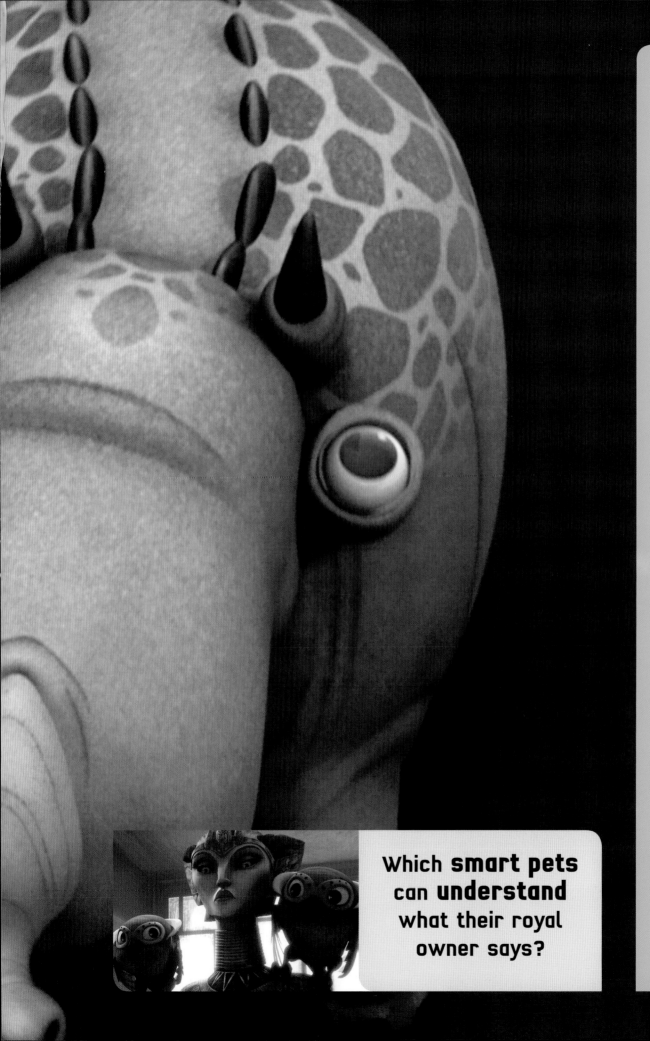

CHAPTER 3

Which **smart pets** can **understand** what their royal owner says?

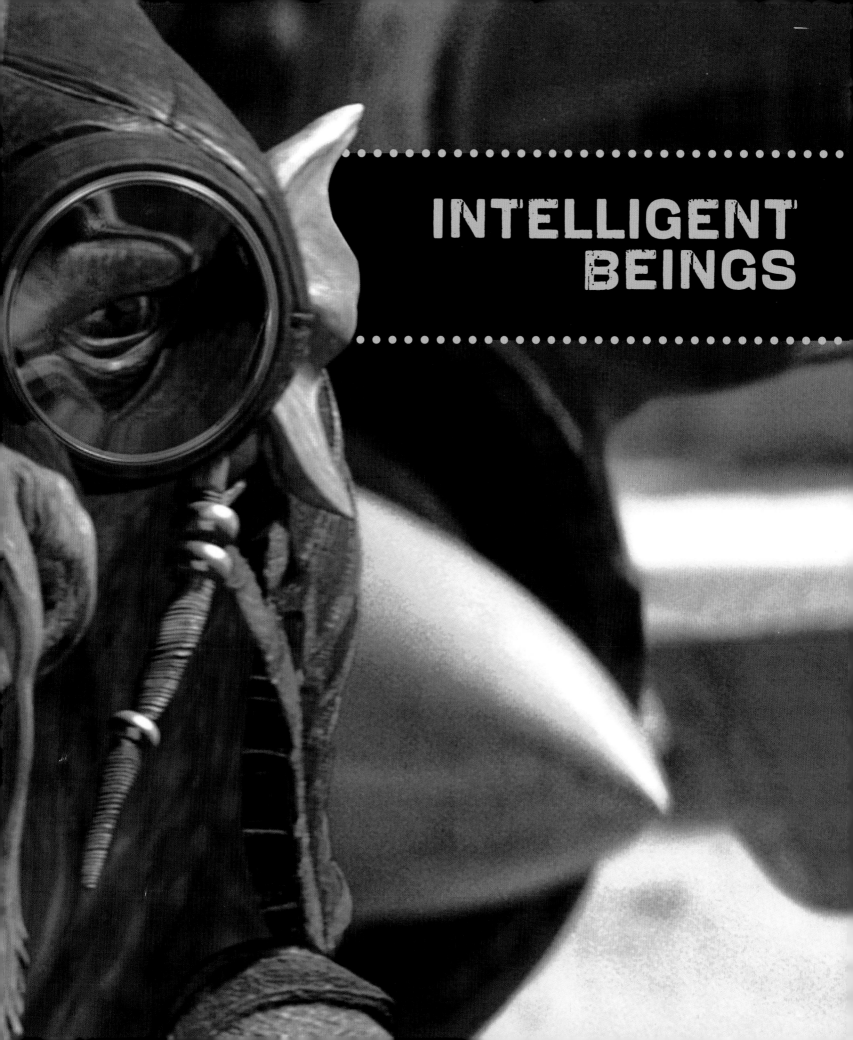

INTELLIGENT
BEINGS

BEST
KNOWN FOR

LIVING IN
TREETOP
VILLAGES

Ewoks

Tell me more!

BEATING THE EMPIRE—EWOK STYLE

Think you need high-tech weapons to trash **Imperial walkers** and bash **stormtroopers**? Ewoks don't! They **roll logs** to knock them over, pound them with **slingshots**, drop **rocks** on them from gliders, trip them up with **ropes**, and smash them with **log traps**! Take that!

Baby Ewoks, known as "**woklings**," sleep in baskets. When they get older, each receives a **hood** to wear and becomes a **full tribe member**.

How to speak Ewokese

"YAA–YAAH!"
"GREETINGS!"

"YUB NUB!"
"HOORAY!"

"EE CHEE WA MAA!"
"WOW!"

Ewoks **don't build fast vehicles**, but they seem to like **driving other people's**! Paploo steals a **speeder bike** to distract Imperial soldiers, while two other Ewoks take charge of an **Imperial walker**.

THE SOUNDS OF MUSIC

1. **Drums**—Ewoks can beat a **mean rhythm** on their animal-skin-covered drums.
2. **Trumpets**—Animal horns make terrific trumpets, and create a **super loud blast**!
3. **Woodwind instruments**—Bird whistles and reed flutes flesh out the Ewok orchestra.
4. **Xylophones**—Not everyone can hit the right note on wooden slats or **stormtrooper helmets**!
5. **Voices**—Ewoks love singing and **burst into song** while preparing to cook the rebels!

Q: Do Ewoks have pets?

A: **Yes!** Chief Chirpa has a pet lizard that sits on his lap—or sometimes **his head**! Other animals must work for their keep. **Tip-yips** are like hens and are raised for their eggs. **Pulgas, bordoks,** and **gaupas** are used for riding.

WARRIOR TRIBE

Small? Yes. **Cuddly?** Maybe. **Tough?** Absolutely! The **furry, forest-dwelling** Ewoks may look like teddy bears, but the rebels couldn't win the **Battle of Endor** without them!

Fast Facts

HOMEWORLD: Forest Moon of Endor

AFFILIATION: Side with the Rebel Alliance against the Empire

APPEARANCE: Cute, but appearances can be deceptive

SNEAKY SKILLS: Making traps and snares out of plants and rocks, ambushing unwary stormtroopers

Peek behind the scenes

Wicket W. Warrick is played by Warwick Davis. His other roles include Willow, and both in *Willow*, and both Professor Flitwick and Griphook in the *Harry Potter* movies.

"Coatee-cha tu yub nub!"

EWOKS SINGING "CELEBRATE THE FREEDOM!" AFTER THE BATTLE OF ENDOR IS WON

In Ewok tradition, chiefs are **always males**. However, Chief Chirpa's daughter, Princess Kneesaa, shows **great bravery and leadership**. She becomes the tribe's **first female chief!**

WOW!...

30,000,000+

Population of Ewoks on Endor

REALLY?!

Ewoks will **EAT** almost anything! They are just about to **DINE ON SOME REBELS** when Luke and C-3PO stop them!

In numbers

200 Ewoks
Population of Bright Tree Village

42 seasons
Length of time Chief Chirpa has led his tribe before the Battle of Endor

15m (49ft 3in)
Bright Tree Village's height above the ground

13 teeth
Hang from Teebo's necklace

3 fingers
On an Ewok's hand

1m (3ft 3in)
Average Ewok height

TOP 3

SKULLS WORN ON EWOK HEADS

1. **Churi**—this giant bird's cranium makes the tribe's shaman, Logray, **look taller than he really is.**

2. **Gurreck**—sharp tusks and fangs make it a bit **risky to wear** this predator on your head! Teebo doesn't seem to care.

3. **Forest beast**—a horned monster's head adorns the Elder Leektar's noggin.

BUZZING SWARM

The insectoid Geonosians come from a desolate world where only the strong survive. Their exoskeletons match the planet's rocky surface—rough, sharp, and hard to crack!

Q: Who is the big boss?

A: **Archduke Poggle the Lesser** is the leader of all Geonosian hives (under Queen Karina). Poggle and his fellow aristocrats are **filthy rich** thanks to his decision to boost production— more droids means **more money**!

How to gesture in Geonosian

"WORK HARDER"
Click outer mandible twice

"10,000 CREDITS"
Rapidly click inner mandible 10,000 times

"DIE"
Loudly click both inner and outer mandibles together

"HELLO"
No such word exists!

In numbers ●●●

5,000,000 B-1 battle droids
Sold to the Trade Federation before the Clone Wars began

8 seconds
The time it takes for the queen to lay one egg!

6 years old
Age that Geonosian soldier drones start their training

5% of population
Belong to the aristocracy

GROSS!! Archduke Poggle's walking staff is made from the **LIMB BONES** of an unlucky political opponent!

Tell me more!

LIFE'S NOT FAIR...

Geonosians have a **caste-based society**. The upper classes enjoy a **life of luxury**, while poor lower classes **fight in the army** or **slave away** in the factories.

102

Fast Facts

HOMEWORLD: Geonosis

AFFILIATION: Trade Federation and Separatist allies

COOL FEATURES: Moth-like wings and toes that can cling to rocks

Peek behind the scenes
Flying foxes squabbling over a banana and the mating cries of penguins were used to create the strange noises that the Geonosians make.

GRIMY FACTORIES

Dug into Geonosis's underground • Maze of polluted, dirty, stinky tunnels • Exhaust vents let out toxic gases to surface • Unsafe machines often squash Geonosian workers!

"We build weapons, Senator... that is our business!"

POGGLE THE LESSER

STRANGE

...BUT TRUE

Geonosians **"get drunk"** by eating a **special fungus**. It reacts with their stomach fluids to create a **body odor** that produces **euphoria**!

Peek behind the scenes
A termite infestation in filmmaker George Lucas's house inspired the Geonosians. He even collected some of the insects in a jar for his artists!

HOW DO SOLDIER DRONES MAKE LAZY WORKERS EXPLODE?

Use sonic blasters to blow up or stun a target.

WOW!...

100 billion
The population of Geonosis—it's crowded in the hives!

Fast Facts

THE GANG: Criminals, slaves, guards, assorted flunkies

THE BOSS: Jabba the Hutt

AFFILIATION: Money and power

LOCATION: Jabba's palace and wherever Jabba sends them

Slaves of fortune

As if being a slave for the hideous Hutt isn't bad enough, you also have to mind his **vile temper**! Jabba's **favorite performer** Yarna d'al'Gargan, and Barada, a **mechanic and skiff guard**, know the ropes. But Twi'lek dancer Oola, who is tricked into slavery, is less fortunate. After Oola rejects Jabba's slimy attentions, he feeds her to his **pet rancor beast**, and takes Princess Leia as a replacement— his **last slave and biggest mistake**!

Oola

BEST KNOWN FOR

BEING LUNCH FOR JABBA'S RANCOR!

Gamorrean Guard

TOP 8

JOBS IN JABBA'S PALACE

Peek behind the scenes
For Jabba's palace, George Lucas wanted even more aliens than Episode IV's Cantina scene, so he spent over **$1 million** creating nearly **80 characters**.

1. **CHIEF OF STAFF**—Bib Fortuna is the Twi'lek who **runs** the palace.
2. **ACCOUNTANT**—Shasa Tiel is the **ambitious, amphibious** Ishi Tib in charge of the Hutt's fortune.
3. **HEAD OF SECURITY**—Ephant Mon is Jabba's Chevin security chief and friend, who **warns** that Luke is dangerous.
4. **JESTER**—Salacious Crumb, a despised, jumped-up Kowakian monkey-lizard, has to keep the Hutt constantly **amused**—or else!
5. **SKIFF GUARDS**—Wooof is a former smuggler who runs the skiffs and sail barge, and is **slain** by Luke above the sarlacc pit.
6. **DOG MINDER**—Ree-Yees is a Gran who looks after Jabba's frog-dog Bubo. Ree-Yees loathes Jabba, but Bubo hates Ree-Yees even more.
7. **PALACE GUARDS**—Gamorreans like Gartogg are dumb, thuggish "pig guards," who do the Hutt's dirty work.
8. **SPIES**—Saelt-Marae is a wily Yarkora who poses as a merchant to spy on Jabba's enemies inside the palace—a job for life!

> **"Die wanna wanga."**
> **BIB FORTUNA GREETING C-3PO IN JABBA'S PALACE**

Saelt-Marae

Ree-Yees

Tell me more!

JABBA'S MAIN MAN

Bib Fortuna is a **"big man"** around the palace. He manages staff, greets guests, organizes events, and even obtains **presents** for the Hutt, like Oola and the **rancor**. But that doesn't mean he likes his boss.

104

Top 5

Bounty hunters in Jabba's court

1 BOBA FETT
Jabba's best mercenary. Legendary pilot of *Slave I*, who captures the elusive Han Solo for the Hutt.

2 BOSSK
A brutish Trandoshan hunter of Wookiees, pilot of the *Hound's Tooth*, and Boba Fett's close friend.

3 AMANAMAN
Mysterious Amani headhunter, who prefers using traditional hunting weapons instead of blasters.

4 DENGAR
A Corellian mercenary who often works for the Hutts.

5 SY SNOOTLES
A glamorous Pa'lowick singer and spy, who executes her love, Ziro the Hutt, in return for a big reward from Jabba.

JABBA'S PALACE

Originally a B'omarr monastery • Jabba's headquarters • Located at the edge of the Northern Dune Sea on Tatooine

"Of course I'm worried. Lando and Chewbacca never returned from this awful place."
C-3PO TO R2-D2

JABBA'S CRONIES

Jabba the Hutt's palace gives shelter to the galaxy's **craziest criminals, bounty hunters,** and **lowlifes**. But don't mess around with Jabba—many who enter this hazardous **citadel of crime** are never seen again!

In numbers

100kg (220lbs)
Gamorrean guard's weight

4 tentacles
On Tessek's face

3 eyes
On Ree-Yees's head

3 fingers
On the hand of Hermi Odle, a Baragwin

2.2m (7ft 3in)
The height of Saelt-Marae

1 eye
On Jabba's TT-8L/Y7 gatekeeper droid

REALLY?!

YARKORA like Saelt-Marae eat all day long to fill their **TWO STOMACHS**. With all that food inside them, they also need their **FOUR KIDNEYS** and **THREE LIVERS!**

STRANGE

...BUT TRUE
Jabba has every good reason to be paranoid. Many of his **employees *are* out to get him**—even his right-hand man Bib Fortuna, his Quarren bookkeeper Tessek, and Gauron Nas Tal, a snarling Saurin combat trainer. That's why he has **spies everywhere**.

105

"My forgotten, da bosses would do terrible tings to me, *terrible* tings if me goin' back dere."
EXILED JAR JAR ON OTOH GUNGA

Gungans don't use blasters. Instead, they throw balls of energy they call "boomas."

Gungans can crack shellfish with their big teeth!

REALLY?!
Jar Jar was once mistaken for **A JEDI** when he wore a hooded cloak. His **CLUMSINESS** was mistaken for Force powers!

How to speak like a Gungan

"OKIE DAY!"
"OK!"

"LOOKIE LOOKIE!"
"LOOK!"

"MESA CALLED..."
"MY NAME IS..."

"BOMBAD"
"POWERFUL, GREAT"

Tell me more!

AMPHIBIOUS ALLIES
The **Gungan Grand Army** comes to the **rescue** of its **amphibious, squid-like** friends, the **Mon Calamari**, during the **Clone Wars**. Gungans are better suited to **underwater fighting** on Mon Cala than clone troopers.

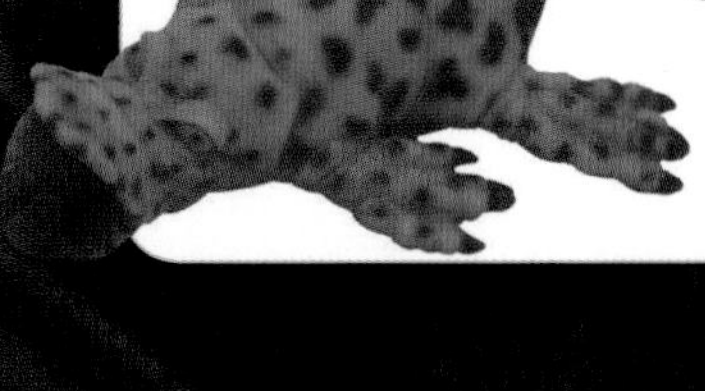

Jar Jar tries to **eat a fresh gorg** at the Mos Espa market without paying for it!

Love interest...
Jar Jar and Queen Julia of Bardotta are in love. The two meditate together by **locking lips!**

106

Q: Why is Jar Jar banished from his home?

A: **Boss Nass**, the Gungan ruler, banishes Jar Jar **on pain of death** after the gawky Gungan **crashes Nass's personal submarine**. His banishment **doesn't last long**, however!

Fast Facts

AFFILIATION: Republic

HOMEWORLD: Naboo

WEAPONS: Clumsiness

ABILITIES: Impossible to describe

TOP 3

GUNGAN SKILLS

1. Breathing underwater and on land.
2. Swimming long distances.
3. Throwing "booma" energy weapons.

I LUV YOUS!

The Jedi Qui-Gon Jinn accidentally **saves Jar Jar's life** during the droid **invasion of Naboo**. Jar Jar pledges a Gungan **life debt** to him, swearing **never to leave his side**. Qui-Gon **quickly tires** of Jar Jar's **bizarre antics**, but as hard as he tries, he **can't get rid of him!**

COOL!! Gungan spit is waterproof and as STRONG AS GLUE!

Peek behind the scenes Classic comedy actors like **Charlie Chaplin** and **Danny Kaye** inspired Jar Jar's goofy antics.

Naboo neighbors

The Gungans and the Naboo **haven't always seen eye to eye**. But when the Trade Federation blockades the planet, **the two civilizations must work together to defeat the droid army**! The Gungan Grand Army **distracts the droids**, while Queen Amidala **sneaks into the Naboo Royal Palace** to capture Trade Federation Viceroy Nute Gunray.

Naboo

CLUMSY GUNGAN

Deep in the **oceans of Naboo** live the **Gungans**, the most famous of whom is **Jar Jar Binks**. As **clumsy as he is loyal**, this **awkward amphibian** is an unlikely **army general** and **Senate representative**.

In numbers

543 Gungans
Lost at the Battle of Naboo

75kg (165lbs)
Average weight of a Gungan

1m (3ft 3in)
Length of Jar Jar's tongue

107

Fast Facts

HOMEWORLD: Tatooine

LEADERS: Clan chiefs, shamans

AFFILIATION: None—they're only interested in profits!

LANGUAGES: Jawaese, Jawa Trade Talk

SNEAKY SKILLS: Can repair anything so it works just well enough to sell.

COOL FEATURES: Who knows? No one's ever seen under a Jawa's robe.

Sandcrawlers really suck! They use a special suction tube to **load scrap and droids** into the cargo hold.

BEST KNOWN FOR

BRINGING C-3PO, R2-D2, AND LUKE SKYWALKER TOGETHER

Jawas

Q: How did Jawas get their sandcrawlers?

A: Mining companies originally brought sandcrawlers to Tatooine. When their mining projects failed, they **abandoned the sandcrawlers in the desert**. Jawas soon took them over, turning them into mobile homes and workshops.

"Jawa Juice" is a popular drink at Dex's Diner on Coruscant (but it isn't made from Jawas!).

SCRAP DEALERS

Jawas are the **scavengers** of Tatooine—they **roam the desert** in **giant sandcrawlers**, looking for scrap and faulty equipment to trade. These **dodgy dealers** have a reputation as **swindlers** and **thieves!**

WHAT'S UNDER THE HOOD?

No one really knows what a Jawa looks like, as they always fully cover themselves— even their faces! Some folk think they are related to the Tuskens, but others believe the Jawas are de-evolved humans, or that they may be even related to rodents!

108

WOW!...

1,500

Number of droids a sandcrawler can store

STRANGE

...BUT TRUE

The Jawaese language uses **scent** as well as spoken words! The Jawas' **stench** helps them **understand one another**—but also makes Jawaese impossible for others to learn. So Jawas use the simpler "Trade Talk" to **haggle over prices**. But **don't stand too close** when they **lose a deal**!

In numbers

80 years
Average lifespan of a Jawa

36.8m (120ft 9in)
Length of a sandcrawler

30kph (18.6mph)
Sandcrawler's maximum speed

1m (3ft 3in)
Average height of a Jawa

"I can't abide those Jawas! Disgusting creatures!"
C-3PO ON HIS LOVE OF JAWAS

REALLY?!
Jawas have a **VERY STRONG BODY ODOR.** They think washing is a waste of water!

TOP 4

DANGERS TO JAWAS
1. Deadly desert windstorms
2. Hungry Krayt dragons
3. Vicious Tusken Raiders
4. Unhappy customers

Peek behind the scenes
Jawaese was developed from African languages, especially **Zulu.** Sound designer Ben Burtt wrote a script based on Zulu sounds, which were re-voiced by actors and sped up to create Jawaese.

Q: Why do Jawas look for scrap in the desert?

A: Not much technology or spare parts get to remote Tatooine. But over thousands of years, **crashed spacecraft and failed mining projects** have left plenty of wreckage and equipment in the desert, which Jawas salvage for reuse.

Want a special-purpose droid? For the right price, Jawas will build custom-made "monster droids" out of many standard droids parts.

Say it in Trade Talk

"MOB UN LOO?"
"HOW MUCH?"

"MOMBAY M'BWA."
"THAT'S MINE."

"TANDI KWA!"
"GIVE IT BACK!"

"UTINNI!"
"COME ON!" OR "LET'S GO!"

"TOGO TOGU!"
"HANDS OFF!"

"OMU'SATA."
"SHUT UP."

ROGUES' BAR

Mos Eisley Cantina

Mos Eisley Cantina is a raucous den of **smugglers, alien misfits,** and **renegade starship pilots.** Patrons from all over the galaxy flock to this turbulent tavern to enjoy **a drink** and **a brawl** over a few **dodgy deals**.

REALLY?!
Muftak is a snow creature with thick fur. He avoids **OVERHEATING** on Tatooine by hanging out at Mos Eisley's **SHADY BAR**, where he can also pick a pocket or two!

Fast Facts

LOCATION: Mos Eisley (major city on Tatooine)

OWNER: Wuher, the badgered bartender

WUHER'S ALLEGIANCE: Whoever pays their bill

DUROS
Duros have **no lips, no nose, green** or **blue skin, green blood**, and they fly a mean starship!

PONS LIMBIC AND BRACONNOR BAKISKA
The bar attracts a **strange crowd**. Pons Limbic (left) is a Siniteen nicknamed **"Brainiac"** because he can **mentally calculate hyperspace jumps.** Braconnor Bakiska (right), is **hyper wary of strangers**, like many of his species, the Stennes Shifters.

ARLEIL SCHOUS
Defel **fortune-hunter** Arleil Schous is getting old. He's slowly losing his ability to **bend light around his body** and virtually **disappear.**

Q: Who runs Mos Eisley Cantina?

A: Wuher is the gruff human who works behind the bar at the Cantina. He may not be the friendliest bartender in the galaxy, but his customers know that he never asks questions.

STRANGE

...BUT TRUE
Nabrun Leids must **wear a mask** on Tatooine, as his species has evolved to **breathe methane, not oxygen.**

NO WAY!!
Dr. Evazan was a promising surgeon until he was **GRIPPED BY MADNESS**. He now practices "creative surgery" that leaves his victims **HIDEOUSLY SCARRED.**

Tell me more!

DON'T PICK A FIGHT WITH A JEDI

Doctor Evazan is **a wanted man** under a death sentence on **12** star systems, while his partner in crime, Ponda Baba, is **a bad-tempered thug.** When these dangerous criminals pull their weapons on Luke Skywalker and Obi-Wan Kenobi in the Cantina, the Jedi **cuts off Baba's arm** in one slice.

110

BEST KNOWN FOR

REFUSING TO ALLOW DROIDS INSIDE

Mos Eisley Cantina

"Most of the best freighter pilots can be found here. Only watch your step. This place can be a little rough."
OBI-WAN KENOBI ON THE CANTINA

CANTINA SHOWDOWN

The Cantina is perfect for **settling old debts**. Eager to **collect the bounty** on Han Solo's head, Greedo foolishly fires at him... and misses. Han doesn't, shooting the bounty hunter dead with his hidden blaster. Cool as frozen juri juice, Han slips Wuher a coin to **pay for the mess!**

HEM DAZON
Dazon is a **grouchy** Arcona stranded on Tatooine after blowing his credits on **salt and juri juice**. Dazon can't get enough juri juice—especially the rare stuff **made from Rodian blood**—even though it makes his **hands tremble** and has **turned his eyes a putrid yellow**.

Peek behind the scenes
Look closely at the bar behind Wuher on the opposite page and you'll see the surplus jet engine parts that were later used as assassin droid IG-88's head!

BOM VIMDIN
An Advozse mercenary, Bom Vimdin is **a gloomy loner** obsessed with his credit balance. With a **sour face and a personality** to match, it's little wonder he's **universally disliked**.

MOS EISLEY CANTINA HOUSE RULES

• LEAVE YOUR DROIDS OUTSIDE. YOU DON'T WANT WUHER ON YOUR CASE.

• KEEP YOUR BLASTER HOLSTERED! WHY ASK FOR TROUBLE?

• FIND AN EMPTY TABLE OR BARSTOOL. CROWDING OTHER CUSTOMERS WILL ONLY END IN TEARS.

• BE FRIENDLY. BUY A DRINK FOR YOUR NEIGHBOR AT THE BAR.

• APPLAUD THE BAND—EVEN IF THEY'RE WAY OFF-KEY!

• MAKE PLEASANT CONVERSATION AND TRY TO LAUGH AT BAD JOKES.

• TIP THE BARTENDER, ESPECIALLY IF YOU MAKE A MESS.

STRANGE

...BUT TRUE
Momaw Nadon is an Ithorian. Like the rest of his species, he **can't speak Basic** without the help of a **vocabulator** to translate his voice.

GREEDO
Like most young Rodians, Greedo has **blue-green skin** covered with **lumps and warts**. Always up for **a scrap**, he scuffles with Anakin Skywalker after accusing the young pilot of cheating at podracing. **His mean streak** regularly lands him in hot water!

In numbers

473ml (16oz)
Size of a standard drink at the Cantina

102 people
Maximum capacity of the Cantina

12 drinks
Available on tap

2 Cantina owners
Since the Clone Wars

MADCAP MUSICIANS

From **dingy bars** to **crime palaces**, the galaxy's favorite **musicians** know how to draw a big crowd. As **bizarre** as they are **talented**, sometimes it's not just their instruments that are **highly strung**.

REALLY?!
Rappertunie spits **PARALYZING POISON** at anyone who threatens him.

Bith have such **sensitive hearing** that loud sonic grenades are said to make their **heads explode**!

Rappertunie plays a mean **Growdi Harmonique**—an instrument that's a **combo flute and water organ**.

Peek behind the scenes
Crew members playing Bith musicians in the Cantina moved to the beat of **Benny Goodman's** 1937 hit "**Sing, Sing, Sing**" while filming on set.

COOL!!
Droopy McCool's body releases a **VANILLA-LIKE SMELL!**

STRANGE

...BUT TRUE
Droopy McCool is a **stage name**. This **Kitonak horn player's** real name is a **series of whistles** that is unpronounceable by any other species.

LEADER OF THE BAND
"Fiery" Figrin D'an, king of the Kloo horn, is the **Bith leader of the Modal Nodes**—a regular act at Mos Eisley Cantina. What Figrin says goes... Well, he does **own most of the band's instruments!**

BEST KNOWN FOR

BEING UNFAZED BY BAR FIGHTS

Modal Nodes

AWESOME!!
Max Rebo doesn't have arms, so he plays the organ **WITH HIS FEET**!

Tatooine's Greatest Hits

1. "MAD ABOUT ME"
   by Figrin D'an and the Modal Nodes
2. "LAPTI NEK"
   by The Max Rebo Band
3. "THE SEQUENTIAL PASSAGE OF CHRONOLOGICAL INTERVALS"
   by Figrin D'an and the Modal Nodes
4. "(THAT JOYOUS NIGHT) I ATE MY MATE"
   by The Max Rebo Band
5. "GOODNIGHT, BUT NOT GOODBYE (MAD ABOUT ME REMIX)"
   by Figrin D'an and the Modal Nodes

In numbers

82kg (180lbs)
Weight of Droopy McCool

71+ years old
Average lifespan of an Ortolan like Max Rebo

21 keys
On Max Rebo's red ball organ

7 band members
In the Modal Nodes

SCRATCH AND SNIFF

Bith have **no nose or toes**. They sniff through special organs beneath the **skin flaps on their faces**! And their feet also smell—**bad**!

STRANGE

...BUT TRUE
The show must go on! Sy Snootles **steals** from her sweetheart and then **slays** him, but it **doesn't harm her later career** as The Max Rebo Band's **lead singer**!

Q: Why do the Modal Nodes dress the same?

A: The band members like to **express themselves** through their music, so **flashy costumes** are not their style. They prefer to dress plainly, usually in **solid, dark colors**.

Tell me more!

DOUBLE DUTY DRUMMERS
It takes **two** to beat out a rhythm on the **massive drum** in Jabba's palace! Drummers Ak-rev (below left) and Umpass-stay (below right) are the **crime lord's musicians**, and act as **his bodyguards**, too.

113

Fast Facts

HOMEWORLDS: Various—pilots come from all over the Outer Rim Territories

OBJECTIVE: To win the famous Boonta Eve Classic race and beat that cheat Sebulba!

MOST SUCCESSFUL PILOT: Sebulba—he always wins because he always cheats

YOUNGEST PILOT: Anakin Skywalker

MOS ESPA GRAND ARENA

Vast stadium for the Boonta Eve Classic Podrace • Holds more than 100,000 spectators • Features gambling, refreshment, and pit areas • Located at edge of Western Dune Sea on Tatooine

Fodesinbeed Annodue, the **two-headed Troig**, is the best-known race commentator at Mos Espa Arena. His red head, named **Fode**, calls the race in Basic, while his green head, **Beed**, reports in **Huttese**.

TOP 6 PODRACERS
(THE ONES WHO FINISH THE RACE!)

1. Anakin Skywalker—a human from Tatooine
2. Gasgano—a Xexto from Troiken
3. Aldar Beedo—a Glymphid from Ploo II
4. Ebe E. Endocott—a Triffian from Triffis
5. Elan Mak—a Fluggrian from Ploo IV
6. Boles Roor—a Sneevel from Sneeve

TOP 5
SNEAKY TRICKS SEBULBA USES TO WIN

1. Insulting rival pilots to rattle their nerves.
2. Sabotaging engines or other parts of podracers.
3. Swerving wildly to force competitors to crash into canyon walls.
4. Using a hidden flamethrower (illegal, of course) to roast an opponent's engine.
5. Tossing metal into a rival pilot's engine to cause it to blow up!

Tell me more!

THE GALAXY'S MOST FAMOUS PODRACE

Have a need for speed? **Professional and amateur** podracers enter the **annual nail-biting** Boonta Eve Classic, all hoping to win a fortune in prize money. Gamblers win (and lose) fortunes, too, as they **bet on the outcome**. Anakin's victory wins him another kind of prize—his freedom from **slavery**.

Q: How do you become a podracer champion?

A: Podracers must be **small and light**, with **nerves of steel** and **super-fast reflexes**. An **extra limb or two** helps, for operating the controls. If you're human, your chances of becoming a **podracing ace** and winning the Boonta Eve are slim—unless, like Anakin, **the Force** is with you!

Peek behind the scenes
The sequence featuring Sebulba and Anakin's battling podracers in *The Phantom Menace* was inspired by the chariot race in the epic movie *Ben Hur*.

DON'T crash in the Laguna Caves—the rescue teams won't come to help. They're going nowhere near the KRAYT DRAGON that lives there!

114

CHEATS AND CHAMPIONS

Thrills, spills, and spectacular crashes—that's what being a **podracing pilot** is all about! Pilots must be tough and competitive in this **dangerous sport**, as they chase their **dreams of glory**—and a **large pot of prize money.**

> **"I don't care what universe you're from. That's gotta hurt!"**
> **FODESINBEED, THE RACE COMMENTATOR, ON TEEMTO PAGALIES'S CRASH**

Peek behind the scenes
Most of the alien podracer pilots seen on screen were digital creations or puppets. Only Mawhonic was played by an actor in costume.

STRANGE

...BUT TRUE
Neva Kee, the Xamster pilot, **flies off course** in the second lap of the Boonta Eve Classic Podrace, while looking for a **shortcut**. He is never seen again and his fate **remains a mystery!**

REALLY?!
Ody Mandrell's podracer **EXPLODES** when a **PIT DROID** is accidentally sucked into its **ENGINE!**

How **embarrassing!** Pilot Ben Quadinaros is left on the **starting grid** when an **engine malfunction** destroys his podracer. He can only watch as his **rivals streak out of view!**

In numbers

947kph (588mph)
Maximum speed of Anakin's winning podracer in the Boonta Eve Classic

66% of podracers
Don't finish Anakin's winning race (18 start, 6 finish!)

18 contestants
In Anakin's winning race

9 years old
Anakin's age when he wins the race

7.47m (24ft 6in)
Length of the engines on Sebulba's podracer

3 laps
Number of times pilots fly around the Mos Espa circuit

0.79m (2ft 7in)
Height of Ratts Tyerell, the smallest podracer pilot

The **Boonta Eve holiday** on Tatooine is a **Hutt festival.** It honors the rise to godhood of famed Hutt **Boonta Hestilic Shad'ruu.**

Podracers have to **watch out** for Tusken Raider **snipers firing** at them. Teemto Pagalies **crashes** after a Tusken shot hits his fuel tank.

"Those Tuskens... are vicious, mindless monsters." CLEIGG LARS, AFTER RAIDERS KIDNAP HIS WIFE, SHMI

WHAT DO TUSKENS DO FOR FUN?

Ambush travelers in the desert

ATTACK!

Kidnap settlers and torture them

Assault rival tribal groups

Capture and care for their banthas

Terrorize moisture farmers

Take potshots at podracers

BEST KNOWN FOR
MURDERING SHMI SKYWALKER
Tusken Raiders

Talk like a Tusken

"AARRK! AARRK! AARRK!"
VICTORY CRY AFTER TAKING A CAPTIVE

"HUURRUGH!"
"RUN FOR IT!"

"ULI-AH"
"CHILDREN"

"URTYA"
"LIGHT TENT"

"URORRUR'R'R"
NAME OF A TUSKEN LEADER

Tell me more!

IT'S A WRAP!
Tuskens **dress to survive**. They wrap up from head to toe in **ragged cloth** to shield themselves from Tatooine's **blazing sun** and **ferocious windstorms**. They also wear mouth grilles and eye coverings to **retain moisture** and **keep out sand**.

AWESOME!!
The most **IMPORTANT TEST** for adult Tusken males is to **SLAY A KRAYT DRAGON** and **CUT OUT** the precious **PEARL** from its **STOMACH**.

FAMILY TIES

TUSKEN RAIDER
Male Tuskens are the **warriors and hunters** of the clan. Their rough wrappings and garments **provide protection** and **allow easy movement**.

FEMALE TUSKENS
Tusken women **look after the camps**. They wear heavy veils over their head and shoulders, with **elaborately decorated face masks**.

TUSKEN CHILDREN
All Tusken kids **wear the same style** of clothes. They cannot dress like males or females until they reach adulthood.

Peek behind the scenes
Tuskens' barking speech was created by sound designer Ben Burtt using the sound of donkeys braying. Bantha cries were produced from slowed down bear roars.

STRANGE

...BUT TRUE
Tuskens are **forbidden to remove their clothing** in front of others, except at childbirth, on their wedding night, and at coming-of-age ceremonies.

DESERT WARRIORS AND THEIR BANTHAS

Primitive Tusken Raiders **terrorize settlers** on Tatooine. Riding **huge banthas**, these **hostile Sand People strike** out of the Jundland Wastes, **slaying** or, even worse, **kidnapping their victims**.

GROSS!!
"BANTHA POODOO" is slang for anything you HATE, because BANTHA CHOW smells absolutely REVOLTING!

Fast Facts

HOMEWORLD: Tatooine

LEADERS: Clan leaders, tribal chiefs, warlords

AFFILIATION: None—all non-Tuskens are targets

STRENGTHS: Desert camouflage, sneak attacks

STRANGE...BUT TRUE
After Anakin Skywalker **slaughters a Tusken tribe** for taking the life of his mother, Shmi, the Tuskens fear him as a **vengeful desert demon**. So they use **ritual sacrifices** to ward him off.

Tusken country
Although mostly nomadic, many **Tusken clans set up camp** in an area of the Jundland Wastes known as The Needles—a **frightening, no-go zone for outsiders**.

THE BANTHAS OF TATOOINE

Shaggy and elephant-like • Ridden and used for transportation • Tuskens cherish them and never harm or eat them (even if non-Tuskens do)

REALLY?!
Though fierce, **TUSKENS** are easily **SPOOKED** into running away. But they'll **SOON BE** back on the **ATTACK**.

SACRED BOND
The **bond** between Tuskens and their banthas is **almost mystical**. Every boy has a male bantha to **train and ride** and every girl a female one. When Sand People marry, their banthas also mate, and should **its rider die, a bantha** usually **perishes soon after**.

If a bantha dies before its rider, its body is placed in a **huge graveyard**, which Tuskens and other banthas treat with great respect.

In numbers

20-30 Tuskens
In a clan group

15 years old
Age that a Tusken becomes adult

2.5m (8ft 2in)
Height of a bantha

1.9m (6ft 3in)
Height of a male Tusken

117

A GALAXY OF DROIDS

Droids of every shape, size, and service operate across the galaxy. From **menacing octuptarra tri-droids** and **efficient assassin droids,** to **essential medical mechs** and **humble maintenance robots,** all droids have a role to play... even if it's not always in the best interests of their so-called "masters!"

RA-7 droid 1.7m (5ft 7in)

TC-series protocol droid 1.67m (5ft 6in)

C-110P 0.99m (3ft 3in)

Astromech droid 0.93m (3ft 1in)

BB-8 0.67m (2ft 2in)

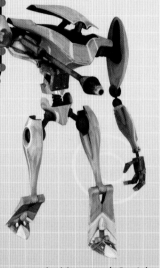

Aqua droid 2.83m (9ft 3in)

R1-series astromech droid 1.94m (6ft 4in)

ASN courier droid 0.3m (11.8in)

IT-O interrogator droid 0.3m (11.8in)

CLE-004 window cleaning droid 0.3m (11.8in)

Imperial probe droid 1.6m (5ft 3in)

PLNK-series power droid 1.37m (4ft 6in)

EV-9D9 supervisor droid 1.9m (6ft 3in)

Firefighter droid 1.91m (6ft 3in)

FX-7 medical assistant droid 1.7m (5ft 7in)

2-1B surgical droid 1.5m (4ft 11in)

MSE-6 series repair droid 0.25m (9.8in)

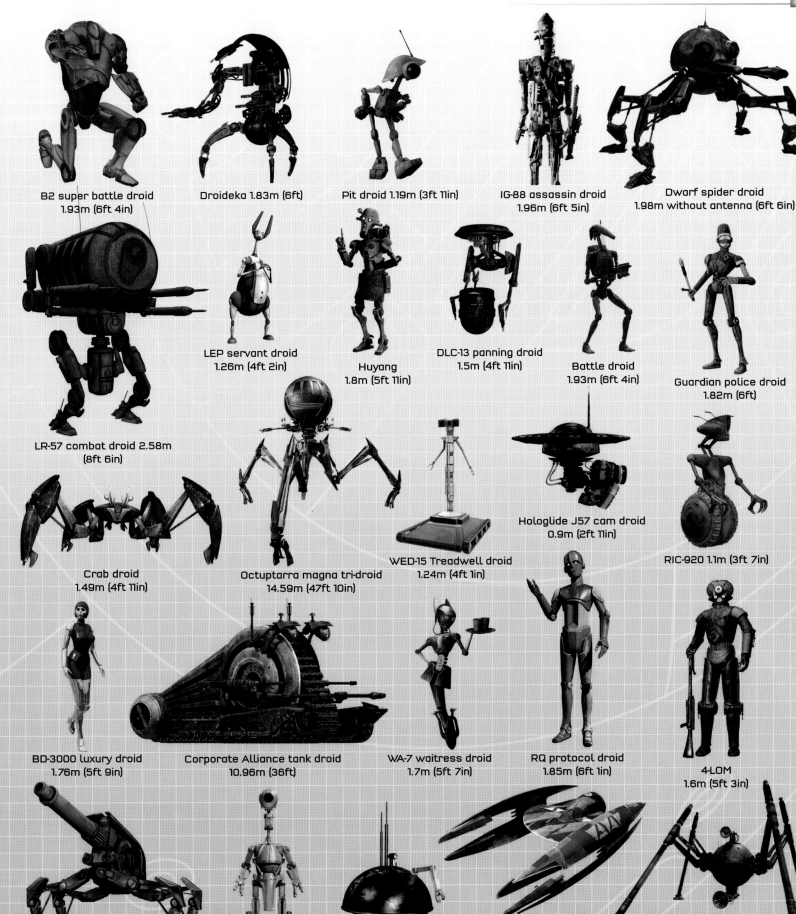

B2 super battle droid
1.93m (6ft 4in)

Droideka 1.83m (6ft)

Pit droid 1.19m (3ft 11in)

IG-88 assassin droid
1.96m (6ft 5in)

Dwarf spider droid
1.98m without antenna (6ft 6in)

LEP servant droid
1.26m (4ft 2in)

Huyang
1.8m (5ft 11in)

DLC-13 panning droid
1.5m (4ft 11in)

Battle droid
1.93m (6ft 4in)

Guardian police droid
1.82m (6ft)

LR-57 combat droid 2.58m
(8ft 6in)

Hologlide J57 cam droid
0.9m (2ft 11in)

RIC-920 1.1m (3ft 7in)

Crab droid
1.49m (4ft 11in)

Octuptarra magna tri-droid
14.59m (47ft 10in)

WED-15 Treadwell droid
1.24m (4ft 1in)

BD-3000 luxury droid
1.76m (5ft 9in)

Corporate Alliance tank droid
10.96m (36ft)

WA-7 waitress droid
1.7m (5ft 7in)

RQ protocol droid
1.85m (6ft 1in)

4-LOM
1.6m (5ft 3in)

J-1 proton cannon
6.46m (21ft 2in)

PK-series worker droid
1.46m (4ft 9in)

LIN demolition autonomous
mine layer 0.56m (1ft 10in)

Vulture droid
3.5m (11ft 6in)

Homing spider droid
7.32m (24ft)

MONSTERS

TOOTH AND CLAW

They don't carry blasters and they can't use the Force, but these beasts are amongst the most ferocious beings in the galaxy. Most people do their best to avoid these terrifying creatures, but some diabolical fiends like to keep them as pets!

Forget monsters—plants eat humans alive, too! Reeksa are giant carnivorous plants that grow on Iego. Their roots are used to create antidotes for the Blue Shadow Virus.

Big and bad!

All these beasts are larger than most species, but by far the biggest and most destructive is the gargantuan Zillo Beast.

How they size up

97m

4.65m

3.7m

1.5m

Zillo Beast
97m long (318ft 3in)

Gor, the roggwart
4.65m (15ft 3in)

Gundark
3.7m (12ft 2in)

Republic clone
1.83m (6ft)

REALLY?!

Gutkurrs, native to Ryloth, like to SNACK ON TWI'LEKS using their sharp, curved claws to snare their prey.

BEST KNOWN FOR

LARGE POINTED EARS AND GREAT STRENGTH!

Gundark

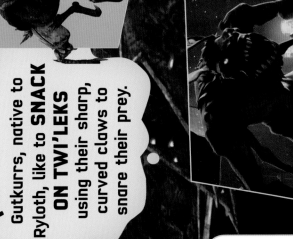

"I wanna get off this planet now. This place is crawling with gundarks!"

BOUNTY HUNTER CASTAS ON THE PLANET VANQOR

COOL!

The Zillo Beast's SKIN is virtually INDESTRUCTIBLE— even a LIGHTSABER can't harm it!

Q: What's so special about the Zillo Beast?

A: There's only one! In ancient times, zillo beasts roamed freely on their homeworld, Malastare, where they devoured the local Dug population. The Dugs fought back and eventually destroyed all zillos, except for one.

Fast Facts

WATCH OUT FOR:
Razor-sharp teeth

COOL FEATURES:
Deadly claws and powerful arms to grab, scratch, and tear

FRIEND OR FOE:
Everyone needs to beware of these beasts!

122

STRANGE

...BUT TRUE
The Zillo Beast has **glowing green eyes** and can see in **total darkness**. It has lived underground for so long, the natives speak of it as a legend.

STRANGE

...BUT TRUE
General Grievous made his pet **roggwart, Gor,** even **more dangerous** by attaching sharp mechanical arms to the giant beast's back!

Q: Why should you run from a roggwart?
A: You need to ask? A roggwart has 20 piercing claws, a three-spiked tail, and a mouth rimmed with sharp teeth! And it's behind you!

Peek behind the scenes
The rancor is described as "a cross between a gorilla and a potato" by Monster Shop supervisor Phil Tippett.

Tell me more!

LOVE HURTS...
Jabba the Hutt's drooling rancor may love gobbling up **Gamorrean guards (armor and all)**, but the deadly beast is cherished by **his keeper,** Malakili. When Luke Skywalker eliminates the rancor, Malakili **weeps in sadness!**

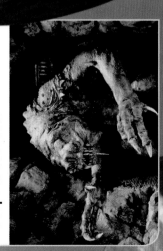

In numbers

1,650kg (3,638lbs)
Average weight of a rancor

16 claws
On a gundark

8 spikes
On the Zillo Beast's tail

2 horns
On a roggwart's head

WOW!...

60,000

Weight of the Zillo Beast in metric tons (132,277,357 pounds)

123

Fast Facts

BIG: Anoobas—up to 2.7m (8ft 10in) long

SMALL: Convor and Kiros birds—0.2m (8in) tall

FRIENDLY: Convorees, Kiros birds, tookas

MEAN: Anoobas, massiffs

POPULAR: Monkey-lizards, Kiros birds, convorees

Queen Miraj Scintel's Kiros birds are highly **intelligent** and can understand **conversations**.

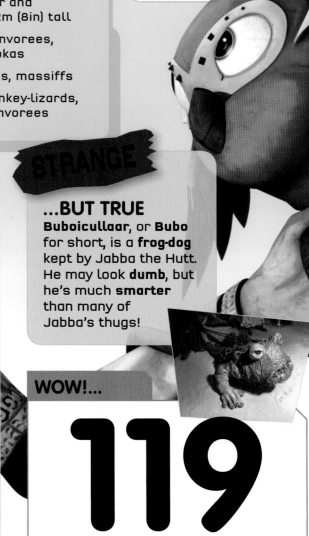

STRANGE

...BUT TRUE

Buboicullaar, or Bubo for short, is a **frog-dog** kept by Jabba the Hutt. He may look **dumb**, but he's much **smarter** than many of Jabba's thugs!

Tell me more!

THE PERFECT PET...

Wild anoobas are dangerous, but some have been successfully tamed. Bounty hunter **Embo** has a pet **anooba** named **Marrok** who is very loyal to his master. It helps that Marrok is **small** and **lacks the deadly saber tooth** that juts out on the lower jaws of most anoobas!

Q: What is the difference between convorees and Kiros birds?

A: Convorees are **gold and brown**, and come from the **Wasskah moon**. Kiros birds are **purple and blue**, and live on the **planet Kiros**. Both have grabbing tails and are popular pets on many worlds.

WOW!...

119

The weight in kg that Bubo can pull with his tongue (262lbs)

PETS

Pets come in all **shapes, species, and personalities**. Kowakian monkey-lizards are **funny**. Tookas and convorees are **cute**. Frog-dogs are really **ugly**! But somebody loves them all.

Tookas are often kept aboard **starships**, where they are very handy for **hunting down pests** and **vermin**.

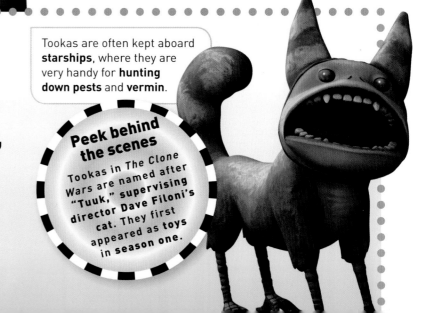

Peek behind the scenes

Tookas in The Clone Wars are named after "Tuuk," supervising director Dave Filoni's cat. They first appeared as **toys** in season one.

124

BEST KNOWN FOR

HUNTING AHSOKA TANO ON CORUSCANT

Massiff

REALLY?!

Attark the Hoover looks like he wouldn't hurt a convor, but **AT NIGHT** he **STALKS** Jabba the Hutt's palace and **SUCKS PEOPLE'S BLOOD THROUGH HIS TRUNK!**

In numbers

60 credits
Selling price of a convor in Pons Ora, on Abafar

35kg (77lbs)
Weight of Bubo

28 teeth
In a tooka's mouth

12kg (26lbs)
Weight of a monkey-lizard

10-12 members
In an anooba pack

4 arms and 2 legs
On momongs and Hesten monkeys

Slobbering blarths
On Naboo, Gungans keep **lovable** pets called blarths. These fat amphibians have **long grabbing tails** with **fine fingers** at the tip, which they use to catch their food in the **swamps**. Blarths have one really bad habit, however—they leave **large, slimy puddles of drool** all over the house!

Top 5

Pet foods

1 WASSKAH CONVOREES
Eaten by **momongs** both in captivity and in the wild.

2 PIKOBIS
Hunted by **tookas** in the Coruscant underworld.

3 ESCAPED PRISONERS
Chomped on by **anoobas** at Osi Sobeck's citadel.

4 GORGS
Gobbled up by **Bubo**—but he'd prefer to eat **Salacious Crumb**!

5 ANYTHING THEY CAN STEAL
Nibbled by **monkey-lizards**, whenever their masters aren't looking!

MASTER AND PET

Hesten monkeys are caught by the **Balnab castaways**, who trap the **large-eared** critters in **nets**.

Kiros birds are raised by **Queen Miraj Scintel**. The Queen of Zygerria has a liking for **fancy, clever** pets.

Anoobas are kept by **Osi Sobeck**, but not just as pets. They also **guard** his **dreaded prison**, The Citadel.

Massiffs are **powerful, dog-like reptiles** specially trained by **ARF clone troopers** as trackers.

Attark the Hoover is owned by **Jabba the Hutt**. Attark is super **smart**, so Jabba gets him to **repair his gadgets**.

GROSS!!

SALACIOUS CRUMB sneaks **DRINKS** from **BIB FORTUNA'S CUP**, and sometimes **THROWS UP IN IT**, too!

Pilf Mukmuk
Pilf is pirate Hondo Ohnaka's **persistent pet**, who **eventually overcomes** Anakin and Obi-Wan after a crazy, failed first attempt.

Pikk Mukmuk
Pikk is Pilf's **brother** and also in Hondo's pirate gang. He **learns fast** and knows how to **drive a mean tank**.

FUNKY KOWAKIAN MONKEY-LIZARDS

Salacious B. Crumb
Salacious Crumb is Jabba's **gnarly court jester**. His **practical jokes** and **terrible table manners** win him few friends.

125

ARENA BEASTS

On the planet Geonosis, the vast Petranaki Arena is the main attraction. Crowds thrill to the sight of ferocious beasts unleashed on chained criminals, or forced to fight each other to the death.

REALLY?!
Normally plant-eaters, arena reeks are fed **MEAT** to make them **AGGRESSIVE!**

The arena hosts plenty of **gruesome spectacles**! You can watch **gladiator-style combat** with beings pitted against beasts, **brutal sporting contests** between beasts, and **staged** battles to **show off** new military droids and weapons.

Fast Facts

SPECIES: Acklay, reek, nexu, massiff, mongworst

ORIGINS: Some native, some offworld (bought or gifted and then bred on Geonosis)

VICTIMS: Criminals, guards, picadors—and other arena beasts!

Top 3

Crowd favorites

1 NEXU
Agile, catlike animal with four eyes, crushing jaws, vicious claws, and a whip-like forked tail.

2 ACKLAY
Part crustacean and part reptile, with sharp, claw-like legs. Tremendously strong!

3 REEK
Has long horns and a short temper. Charges victims and gores or tramples them.

UH-OH!
In the wild, the nexu uses its **INFRARED VISION** to track prey by body heat!

STRANGE ...BUT TRUE
Reeks **change color** depending on what they eat! Arena reeks are **deep red** because of their rich meat diet. On other planets reek may be **brown, gray, or even yellow.**

126

TOP 5

WAYS TO ESCAPE AN ARENA BEAST

1. Scramble to the top of an execution pillar.
2. Dodge its claws so it breaks your chains, instead of you. Then run like crazy!
3. Grab a picador's pike to fend off an attack.
4. Use the Force to control the beast.
5. Hope the Jedi sent to save you arrive in time!

Executing criminals is cheaper than keeping them in prison. It's an electrifying spectacle for the crowd, too. You'll pay a fortune for a seat near the front!

Q: Why are the heroes facing execution?

A: Anakin, Padmé, and Obi-Wan have been found **guilty of spying**—a crime that carries the **death sentence**! Obi-Wan is captured after following bounty hunter Jango Fett to Geonosis and **discovering the Separatists' plans**. Anakin and Padmé intercept his message to the Jedi Council and are caught as they **try to rescue him**.

Lightly grilled **arch grubs** are a **popular snack food** at the execution arena. Yum!

PETRANAKI ARENA

Built in a natural rock hollow • Can be flooded for water battles • Named for an ancient art of combat • Tunnel links it to a secret droid factory

"Let the executions begin!"
ARCHDUKE POGGLE THE LESSER

Pick of the picadors

Picadors keep order in the vast arena, astride their **swift orrays**. These **powerful, reptilian** mounts are tamed by **removing their long stinger tails** and put to use **pulling carts** full of doomed criminals.

Peek behind the scenes

Obi-Wan's **fight** with the acklay was inspired by the 1961 movie *Mysterious Island*, in which a **shipwrecked** sailor battles a giant crab.

WOW!...

100,000+

The number of spectators that the Petranaki Arena can hold

Fast Facts

HABITAT: Naboo swamps and wetlands

LARGEST: Fambaa

SMALLEST: Kaadu

MOST ORNERY: Falumpasets

ENEMIES: Separatist battle droids

BEST KNOWN FOR

"FAMBAA DELIGHT," AN OUTER RIM DISH MADE FROM... YOU GUESSED IT!

Fambaa

GREAT GRASS PLAINS

Site of conflict in Battle of Naboo • 40km (25 miles) from Theed • Fambaa-mounted energy shields enclose Gungan army • Nearby swamps provide cover for Gungans

Q: Which planet do fambaas and falumpasets come from?

A: Nobody knows for sure! Both species seem equally at home on **Naboo and Onderon**. Biologists think **Naboo traders** brought the beasts to Onderon long ago, though **fossil evidence** is thin on the ground.

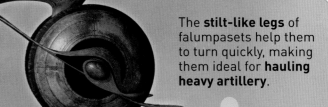

Tell me more!

FROM MINISCULE TO MIGHTY

Baby fambaas hatch from eggs laid in wetlands, emerging with **gills like a tadpole**. Believe it or not, these **plump, soft-bodied amphibians** will grow into the **scaly juggernauts** the Gungans rely on to carry their shield generators into battle.

The **stilt-like legs** of falumpasets help them to turn quickly, making them ideal for **hauling heavy artillery**.

STRANGE

...BUT TRUE

Wild **fambaas** don't stretch up to reach the **leaves they love to feed on**. They'd rather **pull down** the whole tree and munch away in comfort!

REALLY?!

Gungans **LOOK AFTER** their battle beasts *very* well, even housing them in **BUBBLE-PROTECTED STABLES.**

Q: Why are these beasts so great in battles?

A: They **never back down**! The beasts of the famous Gungan Grand Army will **do *anything* for their masters**—even sacrifice their own lives. Raised from young hatchlings, they form very **strong bonds** with their owners.

In numbers

1,000+ beasts
Estimated number of battle-ready animals in the Gungan Grand Army

100km (62 miles)
Echo distance of a falumpaset bellow

10-12 members
In a fambaa herd

6-8 eggs
Laid by a kaadu mother

2 fambaas
To generate an energy shield (each carries one of its parts)

128

WOW!...

100

Maximum number of kaadu in a flock (always single-gender)

COOL!!

CAPTAIN TARPALS of the Gungan Grand Army decorates his kaadu "Swamptoe" with **HUGE FEATHERS** it has won as race trophies.

TOP 3

USES IN BATTLE

1. **Fambaas**—carry shield generators and booma cannons.
2. **Falumpasets**—pull huge battle wagons.
3. **Kaadu**—make the most loyal cavalry mounts.

STRANGE

...BUT TRUE

Kaadu are **reptavians: part reptile, part bird.** These **duckbilled creatures** have **no wings,** but **long legs and sleek hides** to help them move swiftly on **land and in water.**

CHARGE!

The ground **rumbles under their feet** as they approach. These big, bad, and, to some, beautiful creatures, are trained in combat by the peace-loving Gungans for self-defense. So when war breaks out—bring on the **battle beasts!**

Peek behind the scenes
The kaadu snorts were created by slowing down a mix of **pig** noises with the sound of whales spouting water through their blowholes.

4.3m (14.1ft)
Fambaa

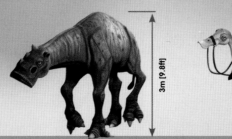
3m (9.8ft)
Falumpaset

2.2m (7.4ft)
Kaadu

Combat creature lineup

Naboo's swamp beasts are **large and powerful.** Best not try to cuddle one—at least when it's **fired up for battle!**

129

NABOO ABYSS

Natural tunnels run from Naboo's surface to the core • The water-filled tunnels are used by Gungans for travel • Fearsome sea monsters lurk deep in the Abyss

Tell me more!

LEARN YOUR SCALEFISH
The waters around Otoh Gunga teem with **seven species of scalefish**—doo, ray, mee, faa, soo, laa, and tee. Some also **live in the depths of the Naboo Abyss**. Humans and Gungans feast on certain varieties, but the great **sea beasts are less fussy, and will eat any they catch**.

BEST KNOWN FOR

ALMOST SWALLOWING QUI-GON JINN'S SUBMARINE

Sando aqua monster

Peek behind the scenes
Early designs for the colo claw fish were based on an earwig. Later, features from a crocodile and a moray eel were added to the design.

Sando aqua monsters are more **terrifying myth than reality** for most Naboo. They have **never been seen** in the wild, and only **a few carcasses have washed up** on the planet's shores.

Q: Why do Jedi travel through the Abyss?
A: Gungan leader **Boss Nass** tells them that the Abyss tunnels are the **fastest way** to reach **Theed**, on the other side of Naboo. Nass hopes the **deadly monsters of the Abyss** will **devour the Jedi** and their navigator, Jar Jar Binks, to avoid Nass getting involved in the crisis on the planet's surface.

WOW!...

54,000
Average weight of a sando aqua monster in metric tons (119,049,622 pounds)

MONSTERS FROM THE DEEP

Take a big breath... we're diving deep into Naboo's **dangerous waters**. Here, **savage sea creatures stalk easy prey**, as Qui-Gon Jinn and Obi-Wan Kenobi quickly discover **to their peril!**

Tiny yobshrimp **live in the gills** of tee scalefish, but not for long. These tasty morsels are **licked out and eaten** by laa scalefish.

130

STRANGE

...BUT TRUE
Opee sea killers **zip** through the water by **jet propulsion!** They **suck water** in through their **mouths** and **squirt** it out from small vents at the **rear of their bodies**, like a natural jet engine.

WHO EATS WHAT?

SANDO AQUA MONSTER eats...

COLO CLAW FISH eats...

OPEE SEA KILLER eats...

SCALEFISH: Doo, ray, mee, faa, soo, laa, tee. And the laa eats...

YOBSHRIMP Dish of the day!

The monstrous sando rules the Naboo Abyss. As the top predator, it eats anything it catches. And so it goes, as larger creatures eat smaller ones, all the way down to the tiny yobshrimp.

In numbers

160m (524ft 11in)
Length of a male sando aqua monster

100 years
Lifespan of a sando

40m (131ft 3in)
Length of a colo claw fish

20m (65ft 6in)
Length of an opee sea killer

A male opee sea killer **carries its mate's eggs in its mouth** for around three months. So, it **must not eat anything** until the young are born!

Top 3

Scary sea beast attacks

1 SANDO
Grabs and holds prey in its huge, powerful arms, before tearing off its victim's head.

2 COLO
Stuns prey with an intense hydrosonic screech, and then leaps from its lair to catch a meal with its vicious claws.

3 OPEE
Clings quietly to rocky outcrops, and lures prey in with its worm-like antennae, before striking with its long tongue.

Fast Facts

HABITAT: Naboo Abyss

LARGEST: Sando aqua monster

SMALLEST: Opee sea killer

WATCH OUT FOR:
Sando: Huge mouth, strong arms
Colo claw: Lethal fangs, claws
Opee: Long, sticky tongue

REALLY?!
If eaten, young opees can **CHEW THEIR WAY** out of a colo claw fish's **STOMACH**, destroying the larger predator.

A colo claw fish can swallow prey **larger than its own head** by **unhinging** its jaw! It can also **expand its stomach** to enjoy a very big fish dinner.

"There's *always* a bigger fish."
QUI-GON, ON THE RUN!

GUNGAN STYLE
The tribubble bongo sub looks like a sea creature. Its hull is **grown from coral** using secret technology, and **tentacle-like fins** propel it along. **Organic bubble-shields**, like those around Gungan cities, keep the sub dry inside.

REALLY?!
DEWBACKS get their name because they LICK the MORNING DEW off their BACKS.

HITCHING A RIDE

In peacetime or on the fields of battle, **beasts of burden** move people and goods throughout the galaxy. From **bountiful banthas** to **swooping rupings**, these creatures prove their strength, time and again.

Fast Facts

HABITATS: Deserts, frozen wastes, and swamps, to name a few

BEWARE OF: The ronto's nervousness

LARGEST: Ruping (counting wingspan)

SMALLEST: Eopie

SMELLIEST: Tauntaun

FRIEND OR FOE: Friend, if well fed!

Q: Why are rontos so easily spooked?

A: Although rontos have excellent hearing and a superb sense of smell, their **eyesight is poor**, which is why they are startled by **sudden movements**.

In numbers

4,000kg (8,819lbs)
Weight of an adult bantha

90 kph (56mph)
Top speed that tauntauns can run on Hoth's icy plains

50-85 eggs
Laid by a female dewback each year

20+ eopies
Live in a herd

14.8m (48ft 5in)
Wingspan of a ruping

BANTHAS— WASTE NOT, WANT NOT

Banthas are more than a reliable means of transportation—the whole beast is put to good use.

Peek behind the scenes
A live elephant wearing furs and horns played the bantha in the original Star Wars. It was later digitally replicated and added to the Special Edition of Return of the Jedi to form a herd.

1. FOOD
Female banthas produce a **rich blue milk**, which is used in **ice cream, yogurt, and butter**. Their **meat** is also sought after for **dried jerky, steaks, and burgers**, often cooked using **fuel** made from **dried bantha dung**!

2. DRINK
Thirsty? Bantha-blood fizz is a sparkling beverage made from **purified bantha blood**! Bantha hides can also be **mashed** with fermented grains to create the bitter drink **Ardees**, aka "**Jawa Juice**."

3. OTHER USES
The **rest of the hide** is tanned and turned into **clothes or furniture**.

Dewbacks are **large reptiles** native to Tatooine's Dune Sea. Well-suited to the planet's **harsh climate** and easy to tame, they are **highly dependable** beasts of burden.

BEST KNOWN FOR

THROWING OFF RIDERS WHEN STARTLED

Rontos

Jawas **love to use rontos** for transportation. Valued for their **loyalty and strength**, these gigantic but jumpy beasts not only lug huge weights, but are also big enough to **scare off Tusken Raiders**—if they don't get frightened first.

Rupings are fast and nimble **reptile-bird creatures** used by rebels as **battle mounts** to help secure their victory at the Battle of Onderon.

WOW!...

90

The average lifespan of an eopie in years, if cared for.

Tell me more!

GROUCHY EOPIES

Eopies are grumpy critters that **snort and break wind** if their load is too heavy. Despite this, Tatooine's moisture farmers depend on eopies as pack animals to **carry them and their belongings** in the blazing desert sun, as they always **get the job done**.

Q: Why do tauntauns smell so bad?

A: These swift-footed snow lizards have **layers of fatty blubber** that allow them to **control their body temperature** and withstand the **intense cold** on Hoth. Unfortunately, the blubber's **strong odors** really **get up the noses** of their human riders!

STRANGE

...BUT TRUE

It's a bitterly cold morning on Hoth and your **patrol speeder won't start.** What do you do? **Leap on the nearest tauntaun** to finish your perimeter check of the new Rebel Alliance Echo Base.

TOP 3

DEWBACK TREATS

1. **Tubers**—in the Dune Sea.
2. **Grass patches**—found in rare desert oases.
3. **Womp rats**—found in swamps, Beggar's Canyon, and the Jundland Wastes.

Fast Facts

HABITAT: Ice fields, snowy plains, mountains

FRIENDLY: Tauntaun, white bantha, mastmot

HOSTILE: Wampa, horax

UNPREDICTABLE: Narglatch, tibidee

"I thought they smelled bad… on the *outside*!"

HAN SOLO ON SLICING OPEN A TAUNTAUN

ICE BEASTS!

Wild **wampas** and **tame tauntauns** roam across the frozen wastes of **Hoth**. On snowy **Orto Plutonia**, a colony of furry Talz breed **fierce narglatch** to survive.

In numbers

150kg (330lbs 7oz)
Average weight of an adult wampa

25 members
In a average tauntaun herd

15 species
Of tauntaun known to exist

6.23m (20ft 5in)
Length of a narglatch, including tail

Top 4

Other creatures of frozen worlds

1 HORAXES OF NELVAAN
Giant blue reptiles with saber-sharp fangs and enormous horns.

2 MASTMOTS OF TOOLA
Massive, furry beasts of burden whose tusks are prized as necklaces.

3 WHITE BANTHAS OF NELVAAN
Large, hairy pack animals with long black horns.

4 TIBIDEES OF STYGEON PRIME
Flying critters that detect frequencies and once mistook the *Phantom*'s jamming signal as a mating call.

SCALES OF HONOR

The Nelvaanians make a **special elixir** from the **scales of a horax tail**, the smell of which can **repel the gigantic beasts** for a year. It becomes a perilous **initiation ritual** for young males to **obtain a horax scale** and join the ranks of their tribe's greatest warriors.

Q: How do tauntauns survive the cold?

A: Thick blubber! Plus, tauntauns live in **glacial caves** and **grottos**, where heat from the planet's core keeps them warm. Sunlight passes through the ice into their caves, **allowing lichen and small ice plants to grow**, which feed the tauntaun herds.

GROSS!!

Han crams an injured Luke inside **A DEAD, STEAMING TAUNTAUN'S BELLY** to prevent him from freezing to death!

Tell me more!

MAKE THE MOST OF YOUR NARGLATCH

The primitive **Talz** of icy Orto Plutonia rely on their **narglatch** for nearly everything. Not only do they **ride them as transportation**, but they also use their **meat for food**, their **skins for clothing**, and their **bones for building shelter and tools**.

HUNTERS AND COLLECTORS

Narglatch males and females only ever gather together in pairs to mate. Although **female narglatch** are **fiercer hunters than males**, they are **easily chased away** from their slain prey by opportunistic males.

REALLY?!

Jabba the Hutt keeps a **STUFFED TAUNTAUN HEAD** in his palace, beside a frozen Han Solo.

STRANGE

...BUT TRUE

Trandoshans are **great hunters** and keep **trophies** such as **stuffed narglatch** and **wampa hide** at their lodge on Wasskah.

WOW!...

200

Maximum recorded weight of an adult wampa in kilograms (441 pounds)

Peek behind the scenes

For *The Empire Strikes Back* Special Edition, new shots were added with effects artist Howie Weed in a wampa costume. A scaled-down ice cave set gave the illusion that the wampa was huge!

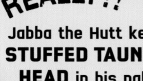

SNOW LIZARDS

Tauntauns have **scaly skin** beneath their heavy fur and **secrete thick, smelly oils** to attract mates. They have **long claws** to help them **climb icy surfaces** and **scrape away lichen**. Their large **horns** are used for **combat** and their **tails** help them to keep **balance** when **running fast**.

BEST KNOWN FOR

HANGING LUKE IN ITS CAVE

Wampa

DEATH BY WAMPA

I. ATTACK
Ambushes and stuns its unsuspecting quarry.

2. DRAG
Lugs its prey's limp body back to its cave.

3. HANG
Suspends its victim upside down to gnaw at later.

4. EAT
Devours the prey at its leisure—frozen or fresh.

Fast Facts

HABITATS: Deep space, asteroid belts

SIZE: Ranges from enormous exogorth space slugs to tiny mynocks

FRIEND OR FOE: Foe, unless you know how to handle the Force

In numbers

10,000 years
Maximum lifespan of an exogorth

1,674m (5,492ft)
Wingspan of the largest neebray mantas

900m (2,953ft)
Length of the largest space slugs (big enough to swallow a starship whole!)

45 teeth
In an exogorth's mouth

3 babies
In a neebray litter

1.5m (4.9ft)
Average length of a fyrnock

Tell me more!

A FRIENDLY FYRNOCK?

While fyrnocks are usually hostile, Ezra Bridger uses his **Force affinity with animals**, and a hint of the **dark side**, to **summon and communicate** with a giant fyrnock at Fort Anaxes. He persuades it to **attack** the Inquisitor and his group of stormtroopers.

Peek behind the scenes
Huge slabs of beef fat and dozens of raw eggs being walked on were used to create the **squelchy** sounds of the *Millennium Falcon* crew's footsteps as they **trudged** through the insides of a **space slug**!

SPACE INVADERS

They say in space no one can hear you **scream**. Don't you believe it! Some of the **deadliest creatures** in the galaxy live in the **wilds of space**, where they **pounce on** unwary travelers.

136

BEST KNOWN FOR

ALMOST EATING THE MILLENNIUM FALCON

Exogorth space slug

The ever-hungry space slugs that lie inside asteroids with **their mouths open** can be mistaken for natural caves. But most pilots only **make that mistake once!**

Q: **Do these monsters only live in deep space?**

A: No. Some species, like **mynocks and neebray**, can live both **in space** and in the **atmospheres of planets**, where they fly around **like birds**. Only a few varieties of mynock live on planets.

"This is no cave!"
HAN SOLO, WHEN HE REALIZES HE HAS LANDED INSIDE A SPACE SLUG!

TOP 4

BEASTS YOU DO NOT WANT TO MEET IN SPACE

1. **Exogorth space slugs**—sharp-toothed giants that will take a **big bite** out of your spacecraft.
2. **Giant neebray mantas**—don't fly through their nesting grounds, or you'll get **knocked silly** by them.
3. **Fyrnocks**—they hate sunlight, but are **ferocious night predators**.
4. **Mynocks**—these **bat-like parasites** chew through a spacecraft's power cables and drain the ship's energy.

REALLY?!

Mynocks **SWALLOWED** whole by space slugs can **SURVIVE INSIDE THEM** for years as **PARASITES**, before being digested.

Mynock on the menu

When properly prepared and seasoned, silicon-based mynock can be eaten by carbon-based life-forms.

Mynock Cloud City and **Mynock Coronet City** are spicy dishes **popular with Twi'leks.**

Professional **mynock hunters stalk and slaughter** these flying pests, to supply space stations and colonists with regular meat rations. Mynock flesh tastes **strong and bitter** to humans, who only consume it when there's **nothing else left in the fridge!**

TODAY'S SPECIALS!

Top 5

Yummy space monster treats

1 STELLAR RADIATIONS
Different types of radiation emitted into space by stars and absorbed through skin.

2 INTERSTELLAR GASES
Invisible gases (like hydrogen) that float between the stars and are sucked through the mouth.

3 ASTEROIDS AND SPACE ROCKS
Packed with tasty minerals and metals.

4 OTHER SPACE MONSTERS
Space slugs need their daily dietary allowance of mynocks.

5 PASSING SPACECRAFT
Always tempting as a last-minute snack or a full meal (depending on the ship's size).

✦ HOME AMONG THE STARS

HOTH ASTEROID BELT
Beware of mynocks and exogorths that live in this dangerous asteroid belt—it has become the graveyard of many different ships.

KALIIDA NEBULA
This magnificent interstellar cloud is one of the main nesting grounds for the giant neebray mantas. Disturb them at your peril!

FORT ANAXES ASTEROID
Fyrnocks and giant fyrnocks now run amok on this strategic asteroid, which once housed the Republic's Fort Anaxes listening post.

STRANGE

...BUT TRUE
Mynocks and space slugs reproduce by **splitting in two** and **growing new creatures from each half!**

RUPING

BEST KNOWN FOR

SENSITIVE EARS AND FOUR EYES

Rupings

In numbers

95 teeth
Inside a dactillion's mouth

25m (82ft)
Wingspan of a dactillion

9 x its own weight
The amount a bogwing can carry

6 eyes
On a xandu

0.8m (2ft 7in)
Wingspan of a carrier butterfly

Peek behind the scenes
Did you know the ruping is named after *The Clone Wars* concept artist Tara Rueping, who designed the creature?

Dactillions used to gobble up the native Utapauns—until they were tamed using fresh meat!

Don't get too close to bogwings—they're very territorial and will **pick up intruders** with their **sharp talons!**

XANDU USE THEIR GIANT EARS TO HEAR PREY AT GREAT DISTANCES.

Can-cells are attracted to the **buzzing sound** of Wookiee catamarans and gather near landing pads.

How do Zygerrian slavers **chase** their **runaway slaves**? By riding brezaks, of course!

REALLY?!
Banshees live on the planet Umbara, a world with little sunlight. The banshees themselves actually **GLOW GREEN!**

WHO KNEW?!
Carrier butterflies serve as **TINY MESSENGERS** on Maridun. They listen to their owners' instructions and **DELIVER** messages to allies.

Tell me more!

CUTE BUT LETHAL
Think convorees look harmless? Think again! These feathery birds **work in pairs** to lift their predators **high up into the air** and **drop them crashing to the ground!**

138

WINGED WONDERS

From the **tiny carrier butterfly** to the **nasty banshee**, these astonishing beasts **swoop through the skies** of strange planets in every corner of the galaxy.

Dactillions live in the **giant sinkholes** of Utapau, but fly to the surface when **looking for a mate**.

COOL!
Gungans release bogwings into the skies to **SIGNAL HALF TIME** at **GULLIBALL GAMES**!

WOW!...

400

The top flying speed of a dactillion in kph (248mph)

STRANGE

...BUT TRUE
Xandu snatch up prey and **smash it against rock walls** using their two arms and two legs. They fly through the skies of lego using **four wings**.

Tell me more!

GOOD LUCK CHARMS
Wookiees believe that seeing a **can-cell** brings **good luck**, and often keep them as pets. The odd-looking creatures are also the inspiration for the Wookiees' **fluttercraft** vehicle.

BREZAK

STRANGE

...BUT TRUE
Brezaks are **giant flying lizards** from Zygerria. They don't have wings—instead they use **skin flaps** that help them glide long distances.

What can swim in the sea **and** zoom through the air? **Aiwhas**—their cool **wing-fins** allow them to **launch** straight from water to air.

CREEPY-CRAWLIES

Bugs, slugs, worms, and warts: The galaxy teems with **creepy pests** that **crawl, slither, and slink** around, **spooking** all in their path!

COOL!!
Duracrete slugs munch on sturdy duracrete used to make buildings, which then **OOZES** from their bodies and **HARDENS** to form their **ARMOR-LIKE SKIN!**

WOW!...

56
The number of legs tiny kouhuns have

REALLY!!
The bright blue slug-beetle from Naboo is a **GUNGAN DELICACY**! These chewy treats are only found under the perlote tree in Naboo's eastern **SWAMPS.**

GROSS!!
Rock warts use their **POISONOUS BITE** to **KILL** a victim and then **LAY EGGS** inside their body!

In numbers

10m (32ft 8in)
The largest duracrete slugs

8 legs
On a rock wart

4 eyes
On a rock wart

1 long, sharp stinger
On a kouhun

BEST KNOWN FOR

BEING JANGO FETT'S POISON OF CHOICE!

Kouhun venom

STRANGE

...BUT TRUE
Conduit worms have been known to **sneak onto starships** and **eat the electrical wiring** while the ship is still in flight!

The kouhun's **SALIVA** breaks down their prey into a **DIGESTIBLE** and **DELICIOUS SLUDGE!**

AWESOME!!
Geonosian brain worms **SQUIRM UP THE NOSES** of their victims —dead or alive— to **CONTROL THEIR MIND!**

Fast Facts

HABITAT: These great survivors adapt to many environments

DEADLY FEATURES: Poison in rock warts and kouhuns, chomping teeth of womp rats

FRIEND OR FOE: Mostly just pests, but some can be deadly

STRANGE

...BUT TRUE
Womp rats **hunt in packs**, seizing prey with their **big, sharp fangs**. When alone, they are happy to **devour moisture farmers' garbage!**

Q: How do you stop a brain worm?
A: Freeze it! Brain worms **hate extreme cold** and can be **frozen** to stop their spread, even after they have infested someone.

On their swamp world Indoumodo, deep in Wild Space, kouhuns **HUNT CREATURES AS BIG AS DOGS!**

In numbers

5 or 6 pikobis
Travel in a group

4 arms
On a momong

2 sharp tusks
On a skalder

1 nuna
To feed a family of four

"Deep fried nuna leg! Mmm, delicious!"
SENATOR ORN FREE TAA, ABOUT TO DEVOUR A PLATE OF FRIED NUNA

REALLY?!
The armless nuna is the only animal used as a **BALL** in the aptly named **SPORT**, "nuna-ball"!

When angry or intimidated, the nuna can **inflate its body** to a larger size!

STRANGE

...BUT TRUE
Ikopi have **hollow tongues** two to three times longer than their heads! They use them like straws, to **suck up water and nectar** located in high places.

Motts give birth to **15 young at a time**!

Ikopi
(not including its tongue)
3.5m (11ft 6in)

Skalder
3.5m (11ft 6in)

Shaak
1.8m (5ft 11in)

Mott
1.1m (3ft 7in)

Nuna
0.5m (1ft 8in)

Size matters
When it comes to **survival**, it is often how big you are that determines whether you're **ridden, eaten, or both**.

Peek behind the scenes
Concept artist Terryl Whitlatch designed the **shaak** to be the Star Wars version of a sheep!

Shaaks avoid Naboo's swamps because **they can't swim**.

CRAZY CRITTERS

From the **hulking skalder** to the **waddling nuna**, the galaxy's **land beasts** are **weird, wonderful**, and full of **strange surprises**!

Tell me more!

BEST KNOWN FOR

BLASTER-RESISTANT SKIN!

Skalders

MOUNT UP!

Wild skalders **aren't usually ridden as mounts**. However, when Jar Jar Binks and his clone trooper allies are stranded during a mission on planet Florrum, they ride the **surprisingly fast** beasts to reach civilization!

REALLY?!

Pikobis can **SHED THEIR TAILS** when attacked. They sometimes grow back **FORKED WITH TWO ENDS!**

STRANGE

...BUT TRUE

A shaak is **so plump** and its legs so weak, it can **barely stay upright!**

Q: What lives on the remote desert planet of Abafar?

A: Not much! Nimble **void striders** with **long necks and thin legs** are native to Abafar. They **run in large packs** across the featureless planet, searching for water.

When a pikobi **hatches** from its egg, it can already **walk and swim**.

HUFF'N'PUFF

The placid puffer pig has a great **nose for precious minerals**... and trouble! Their amazing schnozzes make them a **prized item for smugglers. Don't scare them though**—if they sense danger, they can **puff up to three times** their normal size, and keep going depending on the level of threat!

(WHAT'S FOR DINNER?)

SHAAK—Slow-moving herbivore that grazes on the grasslands of Naboo.

NUNA—Armless omnivore that eats plants and, on rare occasions, fish.

MOTT—Horn-nosed herbivore from Naboo that eats swamp vegetation.

MOMONG—Carnivore that loves the feathered delicacy, fresh convor.

SKALDER—Lumbering herbivore that uses its tusks to dig up roots on Florrum.

IKOPI—Long-legged herbivore that elongates its tongue to slurp up water or nectar.

PIKOBI—Small, fast carnivore that eats tinier creatures in one gulp!

Fast Facts

LOOK OUT BELOW!

Shaaks sometimes **slip into rivers** or get swept down Naboo's majestic **waterfalls**. Their **fatty bodies** help them **survive the fall and float** until they reach land!

SPECIES NAME: Shaak

HABITAT: Grassy plains where food is plentiful

BEWARE OF: Being squashed by stampedes, when shaak herds are alarmed!

FRIEND OR FOE: Friend; these timid creatures are rarely dangerous to humans

A CONVOR IN THE HAND...

Momongs are **mischievous, monkey-like creatures** that live on the Trandoshan moon of Wasskah, where they **prey on yellow convor birds**—but not always successfully. On one memorable occasion, a greedy momong tries to snatch several convorees outside Ahsoka Tano's base on Wasskah. It fails— only to be **picked up** by its intended victims and **flung off the tree!**

Fast Facts

BEST KNOWN FOR

DEVOURING CLONE TROOPER "CUTUP"

Rishi eel

SURFACE FEEDERS: Sarlaccs and vixus wait for prey to come to them

TRANSPORTS: Milodons carry people and goods over long distances

WATER DWELLERS: Nos monsters live in deep, murky water

FEROCIOUS HUNTERS: Rishi eels stalk victims and pounce suddenly

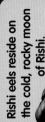

Vixus vanquish prey during Umbara's endless nights.

Nos monsters nest in deep sinkholes on Utapau.

Sarlaccs survive in the harsh deserts of Tatooine.

Rishi eels reside on the cold, rocky moon of Rishi.

Milodons muster in deep crystal caves on Quarzite.

WHO LIVES WHERE?

GROSS!!
Sarlaccs eat slowly. **THEY KEEP THEIR VICTIMS ALIVE,** gradually **DIGESTING** their **BODIES** for **1,000 YEARS!**

"Victims of the almighty Sarlacc: His Excellency hopes you will die honorably."

C-3PO TRANSLATING FOR JABBA

Tell me more!

CATCHING TRAINS

The **Kage Warriors** of Quarzite ride **scampering, multi-legged milodons** through caves beneath the planet's surface. They even use a milidon to catch and board a racing subtram, or **underground train,** to rescue the captive warrior **Pluma Sodi.**

TOP 5

MONSTROUS HABITS
1. All grab food from above ground.
2. Most scavenge, hunt, or trap.
3. Most can sense vibrations.
4. Some can light up their bodies.
5. Many lack eyes or are nearly blind.

In numbers

22,588kg (48,987lbs)
A sarlacc's maximum weight

100m (328ft)
Average length of a female sarlacc

24 legs
On a milodon (plus pincers and feelers)

10 eyes
On a rishi eel (2 big, 8 small)

7 tentacles
On a vixus (plus a long, taloned tongue)

4 mandibles
In a rishi eel's mouth

STRANGE

...BUT TRUE

Baby sarlaccs stay on the surface and only dig below ground when they reach adulthood. While **female** sarlaccs are large, **males** are tiny and live as parasites, permanently attached to them.

The vixus uses its disguised, **vine-like tentacles** to pull its victims into its **toothy maw.**

Q: Any intelligent life underground?
A: Yes. The Geonosians, and the Pau'an and Utai of Utapau. On Aleen, the **root-like Kindalo** and the **mysterious being Orphne** dwell in a **subterranean kingdom,** because surface air is poisonous to them.

VIXUS vs SARLACC

VIXUS
- Long, thin, clawed tongue
- Opens and closes mouth
- Blue and purple tentacles
- Short teeth
- Glows from within the gut
- Rests mouth above ground
- Grabs prey and drops in mouth

SARLACC
- Stumpy, broad, beaked tongue
- Always has mouth open
- Brown and pink tentacles
- Long teeth
- Complete darkness inside gut
- Rests mouth on pit floors
- Lets prey mostly fall into mouth

SPOT THE DIFFERENCE

AWESOME!!
Clone troopers only **DEFEAT THE VIXUS** by dropping **THERMAL DETONATORS** into its **STOMACH.**

WOW!...
50,000
Lifespan of a sarlacc in years

Peek behind the scenes
The Sarlacc sounds were made by combining the noise of hissing alligators with the rumbling tummies of a film crew, after a pizza for lunch.

The Sarlacc is a **terrifying plant-like omnivore** that becomes Jabba the Hutt's favorite pet.

Top 5

Sarlacc dinners

1 POTE SNITKIN
Skrilling skiff pilot and weapons dealer.

2 BOBA FETT
Human bounty hunter.

3 BARADA
Klatooinian slave and mechanic.

4 VELKEN TEZERI
Human guard and weapons dealer.

5 VEDAIN
Nikto slave and skiff pilot.

TERROR BELOW!

Monsters are everywhere! In the skies, the seas, or deep in the forest. But they also live just under your feet, ready to **attack!**

145

Where do the **insect-like inhabitants** of **Geonosis** watch fighting **beasts** in action?

IN A GALAXY FAR, FAR AWAY.....

CHAPTER 4

How does the Empire **damage** the **environment** on **Lothal?**

Which **mysterious structures** can be found all over the planet of **Naboo?**

PLANETARY SYSTEMS ACROSS THE GALAXY

Fast Facts

INHABITANTS: Tusken Raiders, Jawas, Hutts, humans

MAJOR CITIES: Mos Eisley, Mos Espa, Anchorhead

LANGUAGES: Many, including Huttese, Basic, Bocce, Tusken, and Jawaese

TOP 3

TRANSPORT FORMS

1. **Podracers**—very popular with locals and tourists alike.
2. **Beasts**—ridden in the city streets and deserts.
3. **Landspeeders**—hover above ground.

LAWLESS LAND

Tatooine

Life is tough on the **desert planet** of Tatooine. From market traders to moisture farmers, everybody faces **water shortages**, constant **sand storms**, and **intense heat**.

Q: What is Tatooine famous for?

A: Gambling, crime, and slavery, of course! Tatooine is controlled by **gangsters** known as the Hutts during the time of the Republic. Later on, the planet falls under the control of the Empire, but it is still **famous** for being **lawless**!

10 WAYS TO DIE ON TATOOINE...

1. Dehydrated in the Dune Sea
2. Swallowed by the Sarlacc
3. Gnawed on by anoobas
4. Blasted by bounty hunters
5. Run over by rontos
6. Chewed up by Jabba's rancor
7. Beaten by Tusken Raiders
8. Pulverized by Ponda Baba
9. Crashed in a podrace
10. Sunstroke in the Jundland Wastes

In numbers

43,000 light years
Distance from the Galactic Core

10,465km (6,503 miles)
Diameter of Tatooine

304 days
In a year on Tatooine

3 moons
Ghomrassen, Guermessa, and Chenini

2 suns
Tatoo I and Tatoo II

1%
Surface water

Bantha — 2.5m (8ft 2in)

Dewback — 2.0m (6ft 7in)

Eopie — 1.75m (5ft 9in)

Native wildlife size chart

From monstrous to miniscule, Tatooine boasts an impressive array of wildlife!

Peek behind the scenes

Tunisia, as well as **Death Valley** and the **Buttercup Valley** desert in California, stood in for Tatooine during location shoots on Episodes IV and VI.

WOW!...

800+

Maximum speed podracers can fly in kph (500+ mph)

Deadly gaderffii sticks have a **spike** at one end and a **club** at the other. Every Tusken Raider warrior makes his own stick, so **each one is unique**!

MOS EISLEY

Famous starport town • 362 starship docking bays • Much of town lies underground

"...wretched hive of scum and villainy."

OBI-WAN KENOBI ON MOS EISLEY

Top 6 drinks at the
Mos Eisley Cantina

BLUE MILK
(bantha milk)

TATOOINE SUNSET
(fermented fruit beverage)

JAWA JUICE
(aka Ardees: fermented bantha hide)

YATOONI BOSKA
(fermented dewback sweat)

TATOONI JUNKO
(powerful Hutt drink)

HUTT'S DELIGHT
(colorful slurry of aquatic organisms)

REALLY?!
The venom of Tatooine's amphibious **WORRT** is toxic enough to slay a bantha.

How to say "Hello!" on Tatooine

"ARRGH!"
TUSKEN

"H'CHU APENKEE!"
HUTTESE

"JETTOZ!"
BOCCE

"M'UM M'ALOO!"
JAWAESE

STRANGE

...BUT TRUE
B'omarr monks on Tatooine keep their **disembodied brains floating in jars,** which hang below their **spider-like droid bodies!**

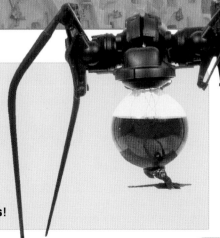

151

SERENE REALM

Wish you were here? Naboo is **an idyllic tourist spot** much praised for its **lush scenery** and **dazzling cities**, above ground and underwater. It's **peaceful** here, too—the Naboo **rarely fight unless threatened**.

Peek behind the scenes
The Theed Palace scenes were shot in Italy's **Caserta Palace**. To avoid damage, Italian regulators ordered that no film equipment touch the palace walls, so the filmmakers floated helium balloons filled with lights!

Fast Facts

INHABITANTS: Humans, Gungans (natives)

AFFILIATION: Republic

GOVERNMENT: Democratic monarchy (human), High Council (Gungans)

LANGUAGES: Basic, Gungan

MAJOR TERRAINS: Grasslands, swamps, vast and deep seas

BEST KNOWN FOR

SUPPORTING THE ARTS

People of Naboo

STRANGE

...BUT TRUE
Temple ruins and **broken statues** are found all over Naboo, though little is known about the **ancient civilization** that built them.

THEED

Stunning city of domed buildings • Set near majestic waterfalls • Queen resides in Royal palace • Capital of Naboo

"We can enter the city using the secret passages on the waterfall side."
QUEEN AMIDALA

WOW!...

14

Padmé Amidala's age when she's elected to rule Naboo as Queen

REALLY?!

Naboo's people **VOTE** for their monarchs. Often they elect young women as **QUEENS**, believing they possess a **CHILDLIKE WISDOM** that is more pure than that of an adult!

"If I grew up here, I don't think I'd ever leave."
ANAKIN TO PADMÉ

Plasma from Naboo's core is a **reliable energy source**. Gungans collect and combine the plasma with **bubble wort extract** to grow their **gem-like cities** and chambers, while the Naboo use the plasma for **Theed's power supply**.

Tell me more!

KEEPING A SAFE DISTANCE

Otoh Gunga's **sparkling, bubble-like buildings** are hydrostatic force fields. They contain **breathable atmosphere** to keep water out, but have **special portals** to allow the amphibious Gungans to **enter and exit**. The city is built by the Gungans to **avoid contact** with their surface-dwelling Naboo neighbors, whom they consider quite **pompous** and **cowardly**.

Q: Why does the Trade Federation blockade and invade Naboo?

A: To **protest against the Republic's taxation** of their trade routes. Naboo is an **easy target** for them, because of its small military and the people's non-violent nature.

OTOH GUNGA

Underwater city in Naboo's Lake Paonga • Also known as "Gungan City" • Connected bubbles allow Gungans to live and breathe • One million inhabitants

In numbers

20,000 credits
The amount Qui-Gon offers Watto to replace the damaged hyperdrive on Queen Amidala's ship

847 years
The length of time Naboo has been a part of the Republic

327
Model number for Amidala's star cruiser, a J-type Nubian

85 sq km (34 sq miles)
Area of Lianorm Swamp

12 people
In Padmé's strikeforce that sneaks into Theed Palace to retake the capital

5 handmaidens
Work for Queen Amidala

"Da moto grande safe place would be Otoh Gunga. Tis where I grew up... Tis a hidden city."
JAR JAR BINKS

153

Fast Facts

INHABITANTS: Many species, including humans

LANGUAGES: Basic and thousands of other languages

TERRAIN: Planet-wide cityscape

GALACTIC COORDINATES: 0, 0, 0

REALLY?!

At a fancy restaurant in Coruscant, just one meal can cost **10,000 CREDITS**—which is almost the price of a **LOW-END** starship!

Coruscant air taxis fly up to 191kph (119mph). Their drivers have permission to **leave the skylanes** and take super-speedy **shortcuts** through the canyons of skyscrapers.

STRANGE

...BUT TRUE

Wealthy citizens in the city's **upper levels** breathe **rich, filtered air. Undercity dwellers,** however, are forced to inhale the **toxic fumes** from millennia of **vehicle** and **factory waste.**

Coruscant is always **growing upward**! As giant skyscrapers are **built on top of one other,** the levels below them get **cut off** from the surface. Some of the deepest layers have been **sealed up** for **thousands of years!**

Peek behind the scenes

As a tribute to the Yoda trick-or-treater in director Steven Spielberg's film E.T., George Lucas added aliens of E.T.'s species to the Senate scene in Episode I.

In numbers

1 trillion+ beings
Live on the planet

365 days
In a Coruscant year

68% of population
Is human

24 hours
In a Coruscant day

Coruscant

WOW!...

5217

The number of megastructure levels that have been built on Coruscant (level one is the lowest)

Q: Is it dangerous to travel in the crowded skylanes?

A: **Not usually.** Crashes are **surprisingly rare,** because most personal vehicles are equipped with **auto-navigation** systems and proceed along **preprogrammed routes.**

BEST KNOWN FOR

BEING THE CAPITAL OF BOTH REPUBLIC AND IMPERIAL GOVERNMENTS

Coruscant

MEGA CITY

At the heart of the galaxy lies **vibrant, glittering** Coruscant. For millennia, **the fate of the galaxy** rests on the decisions made on this **sprawling, multi-leveled metropolis** of a planet.

Top 5

Tourist traps

1 DEX'S DINER
The food's so tasty in this greasy spoon that even Jedi can't resist!

2 ENTERTAINMENT DISTRICT
Streets of shady-looking nightclubs where visitors can gamble and dance until dawn.

3 JEDI TEMPLE
The Jedi Order's magisterial headquarters, which later becomes the Imperial Palace.

4 GALAXIES OPERA HOUSE
Stages magnificent productions like "Squid Lake," at which even the Emperor has been spotted!

5 MONUMENT PLAZA
Where the planet's only uncovered mountain peak can be glimpsed and even touched.

Coruscant's underworld cops are **covered from head to toe** and have **creepy mechanical eyes**. No one knows if they are droids or humanoids, but **everyone keeps their distance**!

Peek behind the scenes
The name "Coruscant" first appeared in Timothy Zahn's novel *Heir to the Empire* (1991).

GALACTIC SENATE BUILDING

Colossal statues outside commemorate Republic's ancient founders • Interior chamber is a bowl-shaped arena • Senators float on repulsorpods to speak to Senate

Tell me more!

THE DARKEST DEPTHS
Sunlight never reaches the **lowest levels** of Coruscant, making them the perfect haven for **scum and villainy. Bounty hunters, criminals, and ghoulish monsters** haunt this murky realm. If you must travel here, **make the trip short—** or it may well be the **last** one you ever make!

"The Senate is full of greedy, squabbling delegates. There is no interest in the common good."

SENATOR PALPATINE OF NABOO

155

CLONE WORLD

Kamino

On the edge of the galaxy lies the **water planet**, Kamino. It is home to the graceful, business-savvy Kaminoans: Great scientists who **manufacture clones to fight for the Republic**.

IT'S JUST BUSINESS

Kaminoans **think the Jedi are strange**! They usually **couldn't care less** about the tangled relationships between the Jedi, the Sith, and the Republic. They never question who is ordering the construction of the clone army— to them **the Republic is simply another paying client.**

In numbers ● ● ●

463 days
In a Kaminoan year

100%
Water on Kamino's surface

12 parsecs
Distance from the dwarf satellite galaxy known as the Rishi Maze

11 years old
Age that Kaminoans reach adulthood

Q: Why is Kamino not found in the Jedi archives?

A: All information about the planet was **removed from the archive**, in a plot to **hide** the clone army from the Jedi.

BEST KNOWN FOR

PLACE WHERE THE REPUBLIC'S CLONE ARMY IS BUILT

Kamino

STRANGE

...BUT TRUE

The **genes** of one man, **famed bounty hunter Jango Fett**, are cloned by the Kaminoans to create an entire **clone army** for the **Republic**.

Aiwhas are also called "**air whales**" as they can swim and fly with equal ease. These **majestic creatures** are tamed by the Kaminoans, who **use them as mounts** to get around the planet.

REALLY?! Clones from Kamino are not born—they are grown in **NUTRIENT-FILLED TANKS** stacked **MANY STORIES HIGH!**

156

Fast Facts

INHABITANTS:
Kaminoans, clone armies

MAJOR CITY:
Tipoca City

LANGUAGES:
Basic, Kaminoan

Tell me more!

SNEAKY SEPARATIST ATTACK
The Republic considers Kamino to be one of the most **important** planets to the war effort, and protects it with **a mighty blockade** in space. The Republic is taken completely by **surprise** when Asajj Ventress leads a sneak attack on it with **underwater assault ships**.

Kaminoans power their cities using the **limitless supply of hydrogen** taken from the seawater that covers the planet.

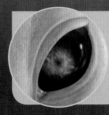

Kaminoan eyes **see ultraviolet light**, which is not visible to humans. To them, their **dull** white hallways actually look **bright and colorful.**

WOW!...

70,000

Light years from the Galactic Core

Top 5

Reasons to visit Kamino

1 LEARN ABOUT GENETICS
The Kaminoans know everything about cloning.

2 SHARPEN A SABERDART
Kaminoans make precision tools and weapons.

3 BUY AN ARMY OF CLONES
Just make sure you have enough credits!

4 WASH YOUR STARSHIP
There's more than enough rain to clean anything!

5 UNDERWATER TOURISM
Take a journey under the stormy seas in a submarine.

Who's who?
Female Kaminoans have **bald heads,** while male Kaminoans have a **white crest** on the crown of their skull

TIPOCA CITY

Capital city of Kamino • Built on stilts above the ocean • Home to massive cloning facilities • Indoor walkways give shelter from frequent rainstorms

"If someone comes to our home, they better be carrying a big blaster."
CLONE CAPTAIN REX
ON THE SEPARATIST INVASION OF KAMINO

157

Fast Facts

INHABITANTS:
Geonosians—made up of Queens, winged aristocrats, flightless drones

MAJOR CITIES (HIVES):
Stalgasin, Gehenbar, Golbah (destroyed)

LANGUAGE: Geonosian

AFFILIATION:
Separatists

6 ways to die on Geonosis

1 Savaged by Petranaki Arena beasts.

2 Devoured by the local wildlife like merdeths and massiffs.

3 Blasted by lethal solar radiation storms.

4 Swept away in frequent flash floods.

5 Crushed by plummeting meteors.

6 Trapped in a factory accident.

HIVES OF DEATH

Geonosis

Geonosis is a **dustbowl world** clinging to the Outer Rim of the galaxy. It is home to the **chittering, insect-like** Geonosians that hunker in vast underground cities to escape the planet's **brutal surface conditions**.

In numbers

43,000 light years
Distance from the Galactic Core

11,370km (7,065 miles)
Diameter of Geonosis

256 days
In a year on Geonosis

15 moons
4 major and 11 minor

5%
Surface water

1 sun
Named Ea

Building for battle

The **huge factories** on Geonosis build **battle droids, vehicles, and weaponry** for the Separatists, who are secretly preparing for war against the Republic. When their plans are discovered, a formidable force of **Jedi** and **clone troopers invade** the planet to take on the droid army. And so begins the first **fearsome clash** of the Clone Wars—the Battle of Geonosis.

STRANGE

...BUT TRUE
As an **insect race**, Geonosians are all born from a small number of **queens**, who dwell in the **deepest parts** of each hive. If a Queen dies, the hive is abandoned.

STALGASIN HIVE
Spire-like termite mounds above ground • Vast network of caverns, tunnels, and shafts below • Capital of Geonosis and first capital of the Confederacy of Independent Systems • Site of major battle droid factory

BEST KNOWN FOR

FIRST BATTLE OF THE CLONE WARS

Geonosis

Count Dooku, with the help of the Geonosian leader, Poggle the Lesser, establishes the Separatists' **secret stronghold** on the hive world.

Factories on Geonosis can extend a **kilometer** (3,280 feet) or more **deep** below its surface.

TOP 2

PASTIMES ON GEONOSIS
1. **Sleeping** (for worker drones between their long, spine-cracking shifts).
2. **Watching** gruesome beast combat spectacles in the grand Petranaki Arena.

REALLY?!
Geonosian **HIVE SPIRES AND BUILDINGS** are made from **STONE POWDER** mixed with **PHIDNA PARASITE DUNG** (poop)!

Tell me more!

A DEADLY BEAUTY
The **awe-inspiring** rings of Geonosis were created after a comet **crashed into one of the planet's moons**. The resulting debris formed the rings, but also left thousands of **small asteroids** in orbit that rain down on Geonosis as **deadly meteor showers**.

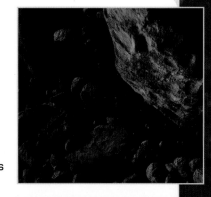

"More happening on Geonosis, I feel, than has been revealed."
YODA TO MACE WINDU

159

Fast Facts

INHABITANTS: Pau'ans, Utai, Amani immigrants

MAJOR CITIES: Pau City (capital)

LANGUAGES: Utapese (Pau'an language), Utai, Basic

AFFILIATION: Neutral, then Confederacy of Independent Systems (enforced)

In numbers

Utapau

51,000 light years
Distance from the Galactic Core

12,900km (8,016 miles)
Diameter of Utapau

351 days
In an Utapaun year

9 moons

1 sun
Utapau

0.9%
Surface water

SUNKEN CITIES

Utapau is a world of **massive sinkholes.**
The **hyperwinds** that pummel the planet's
surface are so deadly that its people
build **underground cities** inside these
holes to escape the winds' ferocity.

COOL!!

GANGLY AND SLIMY,
the Amanis' really long
arms reach the ground,
so they can **CURL INTO
A BALL** and roll along
Utapau's surface!

Pau'ans
once lived on
Utapau's surface,
while the Utai colonists
dwelt deep underground.
The planet's **worsening
hyperwind storms** eventually
drove the Pau'ans below ground
to join their Utai neighbors and
create **combined cities** that
were built into the ledges
lining the sinkholes.

All shapes and sizes

The Utai may be small, but they do
all the mining and heavy work that
keeps Utapau's cities running.

Pau'an
1.9m (6ft 2in)

Utai
1.2m (3ft 11in)

Amani
2m
(6ft 6in)

2 m

1.5 m

1 m

0.5 m

The Pau'ans live for **CENTURIES**, and are
nicknamed **"THE ANCIENTS."**

The Utai, whose lives are **FAR SHORTER,**
are called **"SHORTS,"** which has
NOTHING to do with their height.

The Amani, many of whom are refugees
from the planet Maridun, have **AVERAGE
LIFE SPANS** of around **90 YEARS.**

Peek behind the scenes

The design of
the tall Pau'ans was
originally intended for
the native race of the Pau'an.
The design was inspired
face was inspired
by an African
tribal mask.

Bone people The Pau'ans build homes with animal bones.

PAU CITY

Built within the Pau Sinkhole • 11 levels deep • Capital of Utapau • Major trade spaceport

"There's no war here, unless you brought it with you."

TION MEDON, PAU CITY PORT ADMINISTRATOR, TO OBI-WAN

Top 5

Dangerous creatures

1 RESPUTI
Live in deep sinkhole caves, and love snacking on Utai.

2 NOS MONSTERS
Aquatic reptiles found at the bottom of sinkholes. They're not fussy and eat anything.

3 WILD GINNTHOS
Giant spiders that wrap their victims in silk to ripen for a few weeks, before slurping down.

4 ROCK VULTURES
One of Utapau's few surface dwellers. They can't wait for their prey to perish before eating them!

5 UTAPAUN FLYING SQUID
A problem for anything airborne as it's always hungry and ready to strike.

TASTY!!

Pau'ans prefer to **EAT RAW MEAT,** so freshly slain creatures are on the menu every day.

Q: Where *is* all the water on Utapau?

A: Deep beneath Utapau's surface is a **huge ocean** where all **groundwater drained long ago.** Fresh water comes from naturally filtered seawater at the base of sinkholes or from **machines that extract valuable minerals** from the ocean.

The most infamous Pau'an in the galaxy is Darth Vader's henchman, the Imperial Inquisitor—a cold and merciless assassin, almost as feared as Vader himself.

STRANGE

...BUT TRUE

Utapau's raging winds have **stripped the planet of trees.** So Pau'ans build their sinkhole homes with all kinds of animal bones. Some of these structures have started to look like **giant animal skeletons.**

TOP 2

WAYS TO GET AROUND

1. **Dactillion**—large, winged reptile used to fly within sinkholes or over the planet's surface.

2. **Varactyl**—very fast lizard-like creature that is ridden like a horse.

Fast Facts

INHABITANTS: Anyone who can handle the heat!

CAPITAL CITY: Fralideja

MAJOR EXPORT: Minerals and metal ore

MAJOR IMPORT: Water. Lots and lots of water.

Peek behind the scenes
A real volcanic eruption on Mount Etna in Sicily, Italy, was filmed to create some of Mustafar's lava effects for Revenge of the Sith.

STRANGE

...BUT TRUE
Mustafar's buildings are held up by stem-like **gravity supports.** If you're inside one, just hope that nothing happens to **switch the gravity off,** or the building will **sink into the molten lava!**

HELL PLANET

MUSTAFAR

Boiling lava, erupting volcanoes, and **choking ash** cover the **remote mining planet** of Mustafar. This **hellish world** is the setting for Darth Sidious's plan to **destroy** the Separatists.

REALLY?!
The Mustafarians' **UNDERGROUND BUILDINGS** are designed in the shape of **KAHEL CAVE FUNGUS!**

Lava fleas are well adapted to life on the planet's **fiery surface,** thanks to their tough exoskeletons. When tamed, these **six-legged beasts** make **obedient mounts.**

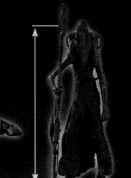

STRANGE

...BUT TRUE
Mustafarians make their **armor** from the **heat-resistant shells of lava fleas.**

Lava flea: 4.6m (15ft)

Northern Mustafarian: 2.3m (7ft 6in)

Southern Mustafarian: 1.5m (4ft 11in)

Mustafarians: Who does what?

There are **two species** of Mustafarian. **Southern** Mustafarians are **short and strong** and do all the heavy labor. **Northern Mustafarians** are **tall and slender.** They often become **guards** and **expert lava flea riders.**

162

BEST KNOWN FOR

VADER FALLING INTO A LAVA RIVER AFTER HIS DUEL WITH OBI-WAN

Mustafar

Tell me more!

CHILDREN OF THE FORCE
Darth Sidious **hires bounty hunter Cad Bane** to **kidnap Force-sensitive babies** and take them to a **hidden base** on Mustafar, where he plans to raise them as **spies**. The evil scheme is smashed by **Anakin Skywalker** and **Ahsoka Tano**, who save the babies and **destroy the base**!

When a Mustafarian **speaks**, it sounds like an **insect buzzing!**

Top **6**

Reasons to visit Mustafar

1 IT'S WARM ALL YEAR ROUND
The climate will be warm to boiling—guaranteed!

2 IT NEVER GETS CROWDED
Avoiding someone? Mustafar is the ideal place to hide out.

3 TOUR A WORKING MINE
Just don't go too near the lava.

4 WEAR WHAT YOU LIKE
As long as it's heat-resistant!

5 SEE THE LAVA GEYSERS
Gasp in awe as these natural wonders spew lava into the air.

6 GO LAVA FLEA-SPOTTING
Watch these majestic insects leap over molten chasms!

While **dueling Obi-Wan Kenobi**, Darth Vader **jumps onto a mining droid** and steers it around using nothing but **the Force**.

> "We should leave this dreadful place."
> **C-3PO TO OBI-WAN KENOBI**

DLC-13 mining droids are made from **heat-resistant carbonite**. That's the same material in which **Han Solo** is frozen!

LABORING FOR LAVA
Floating on their **heat-shielded craft**, Mustafarians scoop **red-hot minerals** from the lava with **giant cauldrons**.

In a **coming-of-age ritual**, a young Mustafarian must saddle up and leap his lava flea over a **raging lava flow**. Protective clothing is **strictly forbidden!**

Q: Where do the Mustafarians live?

A: Mustafarians live in **underground caves**, which are created by lava fleas as they **munch through the planet's crust**. The Mustafarians venture onto the planet's dangerous surface only to collect **valuable minerals** from the lava flows.

SEPARATIST STRONGHOLD
Large mining facility above Mustafar's lava flows • Last headquarters of the Separatist council • Scene of Darth Vader's rampage

> "Go to Mustafar. Wipe out the Separatist leaders. Once more the Sith will rule the galaxy!"
> **DARTH SIDIOUS TO HIS NEW APPRENTICE, DARTH VADER**

FROZEN WASTELAND

The rebels think they've found the **safest place in the galaxy** to build their secret base—the **little-known, desolate ice world** of Hoth. But they're wrong! The Empire soon tracks them down and an **epic battle begins**.

Hoth

REALLY?!

Nighttime temperatures outside Echo Base reach **-60°C** (-76°F)—that's cold enough to **DECIMATE** even the native **TAUNTAUNS** that the rebel soldiers ride!

Peek behind the scenes

Several scenes for Hoth were filmed on location near the tiny, isolated mountain village of Finse in Norway.

ECHO BASE

Secret Rebel Alliance headquarters • Carved from ice and rock • Protected by a planetary shield and v-150 ion cannon

"We'd better start the evacuation."

REBEL GENERAL RIEEKAN

Q: What is Blizzard Force?

A: It is an **elite Imperial stormtrooper unit** that specializes in cold-weather operations. In their fearsome AT-AT walkers, these snowtroopers spearhead the ground assault that **overruns Echo Base** during the Battle of Hoth. They are led by the **bold** and **ruthless** General Maximilian Veers.

TOP 5

DROIDS AT ECHO BASE

1. **2-1B**—Surgical droid who tends to Luke Skywalker's injuries.
2. **K-3PO**—Protocol droid with a memory bank full of battle tactics.
3. **R-3PO**—Moody, red protocol droid on the lookout for spies.
4. **EG-4**—"Gonk" droid that powers ships and machinery.
5. **R5-M2**—Black-topped astromech who helps evacuate the rebels.

STRANGE

...BUT TRUE

Fierce **wampas** often **sneak** into Echo Base **at night**. The rebels trap a few inside a room, clearly marked with **a warning sign**. During the battle, snowtroopers ignore the sign, enter the room, **and are slain!**

164

In numbers

50,250 light years
Distance from the Galactic Core

7,200km (4,473 miles)
Diameter of Hoth

526 days
In a year on Hoth

33% of Hoth's surface
Is covered by oceans

5 planets
Between Hoth and its sun

1 sun
Hoth's sun is blue-white

HEROES OF HOTH
When Echo Base is **attacked by Imperial forces,** Luke Skywalker leads the pilots of "Rogue Group," in a **snowspeeder assault**. Against the odds, they bring down giant AT-AT walkers, buying time for other pilots to **help the Rebel leaders escape**.

How do the rebels defend themselves against the Empire's overwhelming attack force?

With swift, agile, and well-armed snowspeeders.

Tell me more!

DANGER FROM ABOVE!
Hoth is **persistently pelted by meteors** from the asteroid belt that conceals the planet. This is bad news for the rebels. Not only do they risk getting flattened, but the meteors help disguise the arrival of **Imperial probe droids**.

"There isn't enough life on this ice cube to fill a space cruiser!"
HAN SOLO ON HOTH

Top 5

Reasons for choosing Hoth

1 UNKNOWN
The planet is so remote it isn't on most star charts.

2 FROZEN SOLID
Ice and snow provide excellent cover for the base.

3 EMPTY
Great security because there are no other people on Hoth.

4 SMALL
Hoth is tiny enough to be fully protected by an energy shield.

5 HIDDEN
Shrouded from view by a dense asteroid belt.

Imperial AT-AT walker — 22.5m (73ft 10in)

DF.9 Anti-infantry Battery — 4m (13ft 1in)

1.4 FD P-Tower laser cannon — 2.8m (9ft 2in)

T-47 Airspeeder (aka snowspeeder) — 1.4m (4ft 7in) tall, and 5.3m (17ft 5in) long

The bigger they are...
During the Battle of Hoth, tiny rebel machines take on the towering Imperial AT-ATs.

165

Fast Facts

FLORA: Gnarltrees, giant mushrooms, lahdia plants

FAUNA: Dragonsnakes, swamp slugs, sleens, pythons

ATMOSPHERE: Dense clouds envelop entire planet

INTELLIGENT INHABITANTS: One

MAJOR CITIES: Who would want to live out here?

TERRAIN: Swamp, jungle, lakes, lagoons

Q: Why does Yoda say Luke is too old to train?

A: In the days of the Republic, **Jedi younglings** began their training as **infants**. However, Luke is all **grown up** before he learns of the Force from Obi-Wan Kenobi, so **he has plenty of catching up** to do!

Vine snakes on Dagobah will **squirm** and **squish** their way into anything, even the engine of an **X-wing**!

BEST KNOWN FOR

LUKE SKYWALKER'S JEDI TRAINING GROUNDS

Dagobah

Yoda renews his **connection to the natural world** on this wetland planet, which teems with **wildlife**. Here, he **meditates** on how the Jedi lost their way, and **prepares to train an apprentice** who may be **a new hope** for the doomed galaxy.

In numbers

180,000kg (396,832lbs)
Weight of Luke's X-wing lifted by Yoda using only the Force!

50,250 light years
Distance from the Galactic Core

22 years
Length of time Yoda lives as a hermit on Dagobah before Luke arrives

8%
Surface water

1.2m (3ft 11in)
Ceiling height in Yoda's hut

"Into exile I must go. Failed I have."
YODA

REALLY?! The **DAGOBAH PYTHON** that slithers around gnarltrees can swallow up to **15 TIMES ITS WEIGHT** in food!

SWAMP HIDEOUT

Shrouded in clouds, thick with fog, and far from the civilized galaxy, the Outer Rim bog world of Dagobah makes the **perfect refuge** for a Jedi Master in hiding after the catastrophe of Order 66.

Peek behind the scenes
It took more than 100 workers to build the Dagobah swamp inside an Elstree Studios soundstage. The floor of Yoda's home was raised so that **puppeteers could crawl underneath.**

166

Top 6

Veggie delicacies in Yoda's pantry

1 YARUM SEEDS
Make a soothing hot tea

2 MARSH FUNGI
Mash into a creamy, sweet yogurt

3 GIMER BARK
Chew after meals for clean teeth

4 ROOTLEAF
Boil for 10 minutes to make a tangy soup

5 GALLA SEEDS
Provide a handy nutty snack

6 DRIED FLOWER PETALS
Add some crunch to salads

FEEL THE FORCE...

After failing to free his **crashed** and **sinking X-wing** from Dagobah's quagmire, Luke is stunned to see the diminutive Yoda **effortlessly raise the ship** using only the Force. A Force he learns to trust... and wield!

Tell me more!

CAVE OF FEARS

Yoda tests Luke by making him face his **deepest fears**. When Luke enters a **creepy cave** steeped in the dark side of the Force, he comes across **lizardy sleens**, **poisonous snakes**, and a **foreboding phantom of Darth Vader**—whose face is none other than Luke's own!

STRANGE ...BUT TRUE

The **swamp slug** that spits out R2-D2 has **thousands of teeth** in its esophagus—ideal for crunching up plants and animals, but **not metal droids!**

HOW DOES YODA TRAVEL IN SECRET TO SUCH A REMOTE PLACE?

In an E3 escape pod with a cloaking shield.

YODA'S HUT

Built against an ancient gnarltree • Constructed from mud, rock, and bark • Cramped for humans, perfect for Yoda-sized beings • Backup power supply from E3 escape pod • Tiny kitchen ideal for cooking rootleaf soup

"Mudhole? Slimy? My home this is!"
YODA TO LUKE

167

Fast Facts

PERMANENT INHABITANTS: Mainly humans and Ugnaughts

LANGUAGES: Basic, Ugnaught

MAJOR EXPORT: Tibanna gas

MOST FAMOUS ADMINISTRATOR: Lando Calrissian, responsible rogue turned rebel

AFFILIATION: Neutral, then Galactic Empire (enforced)

"Lando conned somebody out of it."
HAN SOLO ON HOW LANDO BECAME ADMINISTRATOR

BEST KNOWN FOR

PLACE WHERE HAN SOLO GETS FROZEN IN CARBONITE

Cloud City

Peek behind the scenes
Lando's costume, with its dashing cape, was designed by Ralph McQuarrie and John Mollo. Mollo was the costume designer for Episodes IV and V and won an Academy Award for his work on Episode IV.

Q: Who runs Cloud City?

A: **Lando Calrissian** is its administrator, but day-to-day running of the facility is taken care of by **Lobot**, his cyborg aid. Lobot wears a **cybernetic implant** that allows him to connect directly to the city's **central computer**. Casino takings, gas mining statistics, and other data are **fed directly into his brain**!

UP, UP, AND AWAY

Cloud City floats high up in the atmosphere of the gas giant **Bespin**. Half-tibanna **gas mine**, half-**luxury resort** for the wealthy, Cloud City makes a unique **tourist destination**!

Tell me more!

HOW DOES EVERYBODY BREATHE?!
Cloud City doesn't need any airlocks or other life-support systems. It floats in a **layer** at the very top of Bespin's atmosphere, called the **"Life Zone."** Here, the atmosphere is **mostly oxygen** and the air pressure, temperature, and gravity are very close to normal for humans.

In numbers ●●●

6,000,000
Bespin's permanent population

118,000km (73,322 miles)
Diameter of Bespin

59,000km (37,000 miles)
Cloud City's height above Bespin's core

49,100 light years
Distance from the Galactic Core

16.2km (10 miles)
Diameter of Cloud City disk

HOW DO PEOPLE CRUISE AROUND THE CITY?

Twin-pod cloud cars are used for patrolling and as pleasurecraft.

TOP 5

TOURIST ATTRACTIONS ON CLOUD CITY

1. Watching the two-hour sunsets.
2. Gambling in the casinos.
3. Kicking back in the luxurious resort hotels.
4. Hiring a cloud car for a stunning scenic flight around the city.
5. Touring the mining operations (for the adventurous).

Yikes! Luke's life is saved by a **weather scanner vane** on the bottom of Cloud City, after he falls through a network of gas exhaust pipes to **escape Darth Vader**.

Q: **Why is Bespin's tibanna gas so valuable?**

A: Tibanna gas is vital to military technology and spaceflight. It produces **four times more energy** than other gases, when used in energy weapons such as **blasters**. It is also used in **hyperdrive** and **repulsorlift systems**. After all, there's got to be a **profit** in it for Lando!

REALLY?!

The **LUXURY** resort suite where Lando first places Leia, Han, and Chewbacca would cost a tourist **5,000** Imperial credits a night!

WOW!...

36,000

Number of respulsorlift engines and tractor beam generators needed to keep Cloud City aloft

STRANGE

...BUT TRUE

Work areas in Cloud City's mining and processing zones have **red lighting**. The **pig-like Ugnaughts**, who do most of the work, **prefer this color**, and it also improves their productivity.

Ugnaughts are **strong and tough**, and can live for up to **200 years**. They eat **genteslugs** and various types of **molds** and **fungi** grown in dark, dank side tunnels off their main living areas. Ugnaught kids are known as **"Ugletts."**

Peek behind the scenes
Ugnaught voices were created from recordings of the yips of arctic fox pups with their mother.

Cloud City has 392 levels • Top 50 levels are luxury resort • Famous casinos include "Yarith Bespin" and "Pair O'Dice" • Lowest levels used for mining and processing gas

Fast Facts

NATIVE PEOPLE:
Ewoks (forest people),
Yuzzum (plains people)

MAJOR CITIES:
None; inhabitants live
in tribal villages

LANGUAGES:
Ewokese, Yuzzum

AFFILIATION:
Neutral, though occupied
by Imperial forces

Bright Tree
Ewok village

EWOK VILLAGE VISITOR GUIDE

GETTING AROUND

It's easy to get from A to B in an Ewok village, if you have a good head for heights. Just don't look down!

- Suspension bridges—hold tight, they can sway a lot.
- Rope ladders—strong but rough on the hands.
- Swinging vines—don't let go at the wrong moment!
- Wooden catwalks—often spiral around trees, so go slow or you could get dizzy.

FOREST MOON

Secluded and faraway, the "Forest Moon" of **Endor** is home to the **fierce, furry Ewoks.** This **leafy, low tech world** becomes the unlikely scene of the **Empire's downfall,** leading to the **destruction of Death Star II** and the **Emperor,** too!

The Ewoks use **booby traps** to snare the **huge, bear-like goraxes** that prey on them. They cleverly **adapt the traps** to **help rebel commandos** defeat the **Imperial forces** on Endor.

Peek behind the scenes
The Endor scenes were filmed in the **giant redwood** forests of northern California, in particular **Tall Trees Redwood Grove** and other forests near the remote town of **Smith River.**

In numbers

43,300 light years
Distance from the Galactic Core

4,900km (3,045 miles)
Diameter of Endor

402 days
In an Endor year

8%
Surface water

2 suns
Endor I and II

Death Star shield

Q: Why is Endor important?

A: The **Empire** is building **Death Star II** right above Endor, and protecting it with an **energy shield** generated from the moon's surface. Despite falling into a **trap set by the Emperor,** the **Rebel Alliance** succeeds in bringing down Death Star II and the Emperor, **freeing the galaxy** from Imperial control.

Ewok

Hunting high and low

Ewok glider

STRANGE

...BUT TRUE
Yuzzum use only
the most **basic tools**. Ewoks,
however, have an **advanced
stone-age technology**.
They even build **hang gliders**
with **animal skin wings**!

NO WAY!!
Ewoks are **INTELLIGENT**
beings, but that doesn't stop
OFFWORLD RAIDERS
from hunting them down to
make **EWOK JERKY**,
a popular snack on
Outer Rim worlds.

SHIELD GENERATOR STATION

Imperial outpost on Endor • Deflector shield protects Death Star II while it is under construction • Bunker houses crew and power facilities

"The shield must be deactivated if any attack is attempted."
REBEL ADMIRAL ACKBAR

Yuzzum love **roasted "ruggers"**—rodents that hide in tall grasses—but first they have to catch them! To help them in the hunt, they tame and ride the **scary, swift,** and **spider-like rakazzak beasts**.

Yuzzum

Yuzzum are **taller** than Ewoks, thanks to their **rangy limbs**. On the plains, long legs help you **run fast** to catch prey, but in dense woodlands, **small is better**.

Boy, **can Yuzzum sing**! Joh Yowza's **gritty, soulful voice** delights **Jabba the Hutt** when Yowza performs at his palace as part of **Max Rebo's band**.

171

Fast Facts

INHABITANTS:
Humans, Xexto, Ithorians, Rodians, Aqualish, Gotals, Ugnaughts

CITIES AND TOWNS:
Capital City, Kothal, Jalath, Jhothal, Monad Outpost, Tarkintown

LANGUAGES: Basic, Huttese, Aqualish, Ithorian

STRANGE

...BUT TRUE
If you see **IG-RM** droids **lurking** around the streets of Capital City, then stay away. These **thug droids** are owned by local gangsters like Cikatro Vizago, and are sent to do their **dirty work!**

Lothal's loathsome leaders

Lothal's governor, **Arihnda Pryce,** is rarely seen in public. The **cruel Imperial military** take **center stage** to run the world's affairs.

Wilhuff Tarkin—proud and heartless governor of the Outer Rim Territories (including Lothal).

Maketh Tua—naïve government minister who stands in for Governor Pryce.

Cumberlayne Aresko—snobby **commandant** who manages military operations on Lothal.

Myles Grint—dumb and brutish **bully** who helps Aresko run the Imperial Academy.

Top 5

Ways the Empire controls Lothal

WHAT'S THE EASIEST WAY TO TRAVEL TO NEARBY WORLDS LIKE GAREL?

Jump on a Star Commuter 2000 shuttle!

1 POLITICAL PRISONERS
Anyone who publicly opposes the Empire is taken away.

2 BRIBES
Citizens are forced to pay corrupt stormtroopers and officers—or suffer.

3 EVICTING CITIZENS
The Empire forces farmers to leave so it can steal their land.

4 EXPLOITING RESOURCES
The Empire digs for metal and rare minerals, damaging the environment with filthy mines.

5 MANUFACTURING ARMIES
Sienar Fleet Systems' factories build TIE fighters—and also pollute the air and water.

CAPTIVE TERRITORY

Lothal

Lothal was a **quiet, green, and pleasant** backwater until the Empire arrived to **seize land** and **deny freedom** to the planet's citizens. Now anyone speaking out against the Empire is **arrested** by stormtroopers!

Peek behind the scenes
Disneyland's "Star Tours" ride inspired the shuttle between Lothal and Garel. The **RX-24 droid who drives** both is voiced by the same actor, Paul Reubens, best known as Pee Wee Herman!

172

BLACK MARKET BLUES

The Empire's **cripplingly high taxes** create a **booming black market** in Capital City. Corrupt Imperial officials take advantage of the situation, **squeezing protection money** from Lothal's already hard-pressed citizens.

Tell me more!

FROM RICHES TO RAGS

Tangletown was a **thriving farming community** that grew fruits and vegetables. And then Governor Tarkin arrived, and forcibly took all the arable land for the Empire and its business buddies. The local people were forced to live in a **poor and dirty slum** they named **"Tarkintown."**

REALLY?! Sometimes Lothal's Imperial Academy cadets **MYSTERIOUSLY VANISH!** Zare Leonis fears his sister has been taken from there by the Inquisitor!

EZRA'S TOP 3

CAPITAL CITY HAUNTS

1. **Bazaar**—an open market where pockets are ripe for the picking.
2. **Sewers**—few Imperials will follow Ezra into these stinky tunnels, in case they mess up their uniforms.
3. **Imperial Academy**—no better place to snatch stormtrooper helmets!

Q: Where's the best rebel hideout in Capital City?

A: You could try your luck up in E-272, the **abandoned** communications **tower** that Ezra calls home, on the outskirts of the city. Just don't touch his **prized** stormtrooper helmet **collection**!

In numbers

3258 LY
The year the Empire is founded (in the Lothal Calendar)

125 credits
For the Meal of the Day at Bistro Lothal

25 credits
For an advance ticket to the gladiator match at the abandoned mining facility, Monad Outpost

20km (12 miles)
Distance from Capital City to Monad Outpost

5 years
The timescale of the Empire's secret master plan for Lothal

4 credits
Cost of a single trip on Capital City's Empire Monoshuttle

2 moons
Orbiting Lothal

OLD JHO'S PIT STOP

Cantina in Jhothal serving local food and drink • Owned by Old Jho, an Ithorian • Hangout for *Ghost*'s crew • Unfriendly toward the Empire!

Old Jho

173

SPACE STATIONS, STARSHIPS, AND SPACE TRAVEL

FULL THROTTLE!

Have a **need for speed**? The galaxy is buzzing with high-powered spacecraft. From the **mighty but slow-moving Imperial Star Destroyer,** to the **zippy and agile A-wing,** there's a starship to suit every mission!

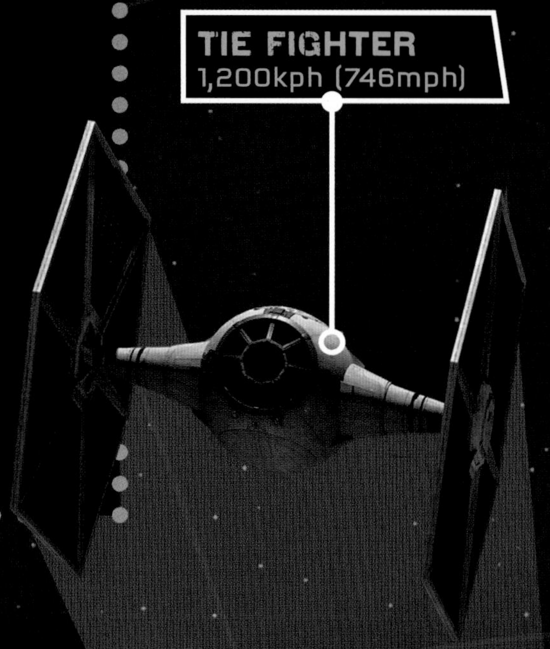

TIE FIGHTER
1,200kph (746mph)

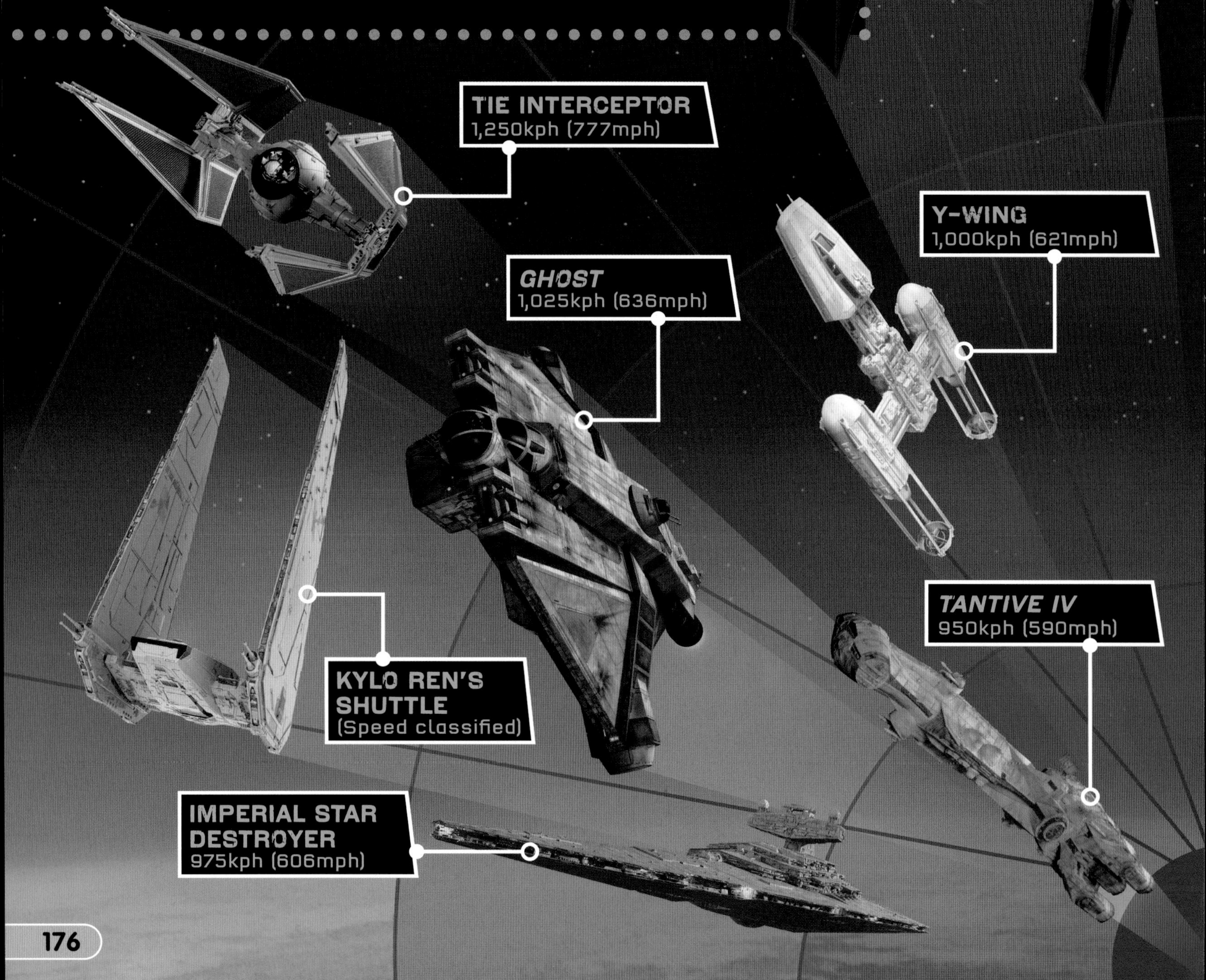

TIE INTERCEPTOR
1,250kph (777mph)

Y-WING
1,000kph (621mph)

GHOST
1,025kph (636mph)

KYLO REN'S SHUTTLE
(Speed classified)

TANTIVE IV
950kph (590mph)

IMPERIAL STAR DESTROYER
975kph (606mph)

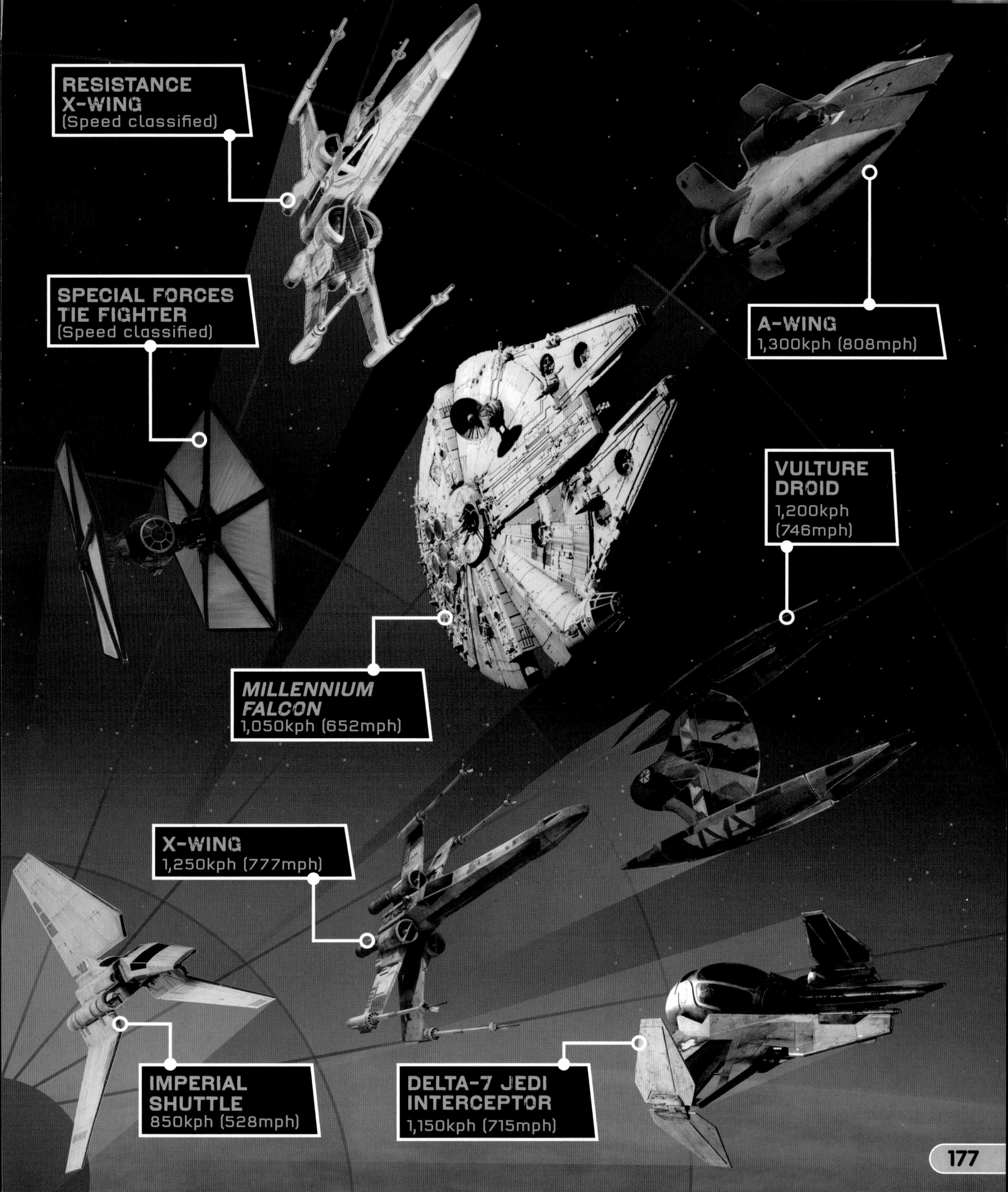

RESISTANCE X-WING
(Speed classified)

SPECIAL FORCES TIE FIGHTER
(Speed classified)

A-WING
1,300kph (808mph)

VULTURE DROID
1,200kph (746mph)

MILLENNIUM FALCON
1,050kph (652mph)

X-WING
1,250kph (777mph)

IMPERIAL SHUTTLE
850kph (528mph)

DELTA-7 JEDI INTERCEPTOR
1,150kph (715mph)

150,000 light years
Travel range of a Jedi interceptor using a hyperdrive booster ring

3,600G
Maximum acceleration of a tri-fighter in open space

1,500 vulture droids
Carried on a Trade Federation battleship

192 V-wing starfighters
Carried on a *Venator*-class Star Destroyer

V-19 Torrent starfighter
6m (19ft 8in)
> Missiles with onboard targeting intelligence.

REALLY?!
The tri-fighter's three-armed design mimics the **SKULL FEATURES** of a **FEROCIOUS PREDATOR** native to the planet Colla IV.

Droid tri-fighter
5.4m (17ft 8in)
> Smallest starfighter in either fleet.

Aggressive ReConnaissance (ARC)-170
12.71m (41ft 8in)
> **Hyperdrive equipped**, largest crew.

Delta-7 *Aethersprite* Jedi starfighter
8m (26ft 2in)
> Interstellar travel with **hyperdrive**.

ARC OF AGGRESSION
Most Republic starfighters are single-pilot craft—small, nimble, and fast—but they lack heavy weapons, shields, and hyperdrives. The **ARC-170 is different**. Designed for **long-range solo combat**, it is large, well armed, lightspeed enabled, and requires a crew of three: a pilot, copilot, and tail-gunner.

HOW DO SMALL JEDI STARFIGHTERS CROSS INTERSTELLAR DISTANCES?

They engage the specially-fitted Syliure hyperdrive booster ring.

AERIAL COMBAT!

You're a Jedi pilot separated from your squadron and under heavy vulture droid fire. You're **outnumbered, outgunned**, and **almost out of luck**. Good thing you just serviced your **superfast Jedi interceptor**.

Q: Why are Jedi starfighters the smallest ships in the Republic fleet?

A: The Jedi pilots' Force-enhanced abilities means they need **fewer controls, instruments, or sensors** than a regulation clone pilot. They also waste less ammunition, thanks to their precision targeting skills. Despite their size, they are just **as deadly as clone fighters**.

Buzz droid
0.25m (10in) (in sphere mode)
> Sabotage droid launched by tri-fighters.

Eta-2

Eta-2 Actis Jedi interceptor
5.47m (17ft 11in)
> **Fastest** starfighter in either fleet.

TOP 4

REASONS TO DEPLOY DROID STARFIGHTERS

1. Can make **extreme maneuvers** that would crush the sturdiest living pilot.
2. No life-support systems allows **more room for armaments and fuel**.
3. **No moral concerns** on certain death missions.
4. Designed for **multiple roles**, such as space fighter and ground walker.

Tell me more!

SMART SHIPS

Droid starfighters were **originally remote-controlled**, but later fitted with **artificial intelligence**. While tri-fighters are smarter than vulture droids and hyena bombers, no amount of droid programming can outthink a clone or Jedi pilot. Droid pilots rely on **speed** and **overwhelming numbers** to win the day.

Vulture droid
6.96m (22ft 10in) (flight configuration)
> Transforms into **walking patrol droid** to assist with ground operations.

Vulture droids are built in the **cathedral factories** of Xi Char, where precision manufacturing is an act of **religious worship**.

Peek behind the scenes
The design of the V-19 Torrent's engines and folding wings is based on that of the F4U Corsair aircraft flown in World War II.

STRANGE

...BUT TRUE
Some Separatist **missiles** don't hit their target. Instead they burst open to unleash the **brutal buzz droids** that **rip apart ships** —with the **pilot still inside!**

Buzz droid

Q: How do you defeat a buzz droid?

A: **Zap its center eye!** This sends a chain reaction through the whole droid that **shuts it down**.

Q: Where does the *Ghost* get its name?

A: Hera equips the ship with **stealth systems** that reduce its energy emissions to make it **almost invisible**, like a ghost! Enemy sensors often **mistake** the freighter for cosmic radiation or a strange solar wave.

COOL!! The *Ghost's* weapons pack a **WALLOP**— enough to bring down a **LIGHT CRUISER!**

WOW!...

87

The number of illegal upgrades to the *Ghost's* stealth systems

STRANGE **...BUT TRUE**
Whenever Chopper sends commands to the *Ghost's* navicomputer, the two machines get into **angry data arguments** with each other. The *Ghost* finds Chopper very **rude and pushy!**

TOP 5

PLACES EZRA HIDES ON THE *GHOST* AFTER PLAYING JOKES ON ZEB
1. Cargo bay locker
2. Inside the *Phantom*
3. Interior air ducts
4. Under the common room's dejarik chess table
5. In Kanan's cabin

Common room

How do you turn two starships into one? The *Phantom's* docking mechanism allows it to attach quickly to the top of the *Ghost* and ride its mothership through space.

Fast Facts

MAIN FREIGHTER:
The *Ghost*

ATTACHED SHUTTLE:
The *Phantom*

WEAPONRY:
Ghost: 1 dorsal laser turret, 2 forward laser turrets
Phantom: 1 dorsal laser turret, 1 twin laser cannon

CAPTAIN: Hera Syndulla

MANUFACTURER:
Corellian Shipyards

TOP 5 STARSHIP FEATS...

1 The *Ghost* uses its stealth systems to slip unnoticed into the Star Destroyer *Lawbringer's* hangar bay.

2 The *Phantom* survives the fyrnock-infested Fort Anaxes asteroid—twice!

3 The *Ghost* provides cover fire during the rebels' rescue of Wookiee slaves on Kessel

4 The *Phantom* infiltrates the Imperial prison on Stygeon Prime without being detected.

5 The *Ghost*, piloted by the mysterious Fulcrum, suddenly joins the fight above Mustafar in the nick of time to save the rebels.

"*Ghost* to Spectre-5. We're in position."

HERA ABOUT TO PICK UP SABINE AFTER SHE WREAKS HAVOC AT A TIE FIGHTER BASE

Peek behind the scenes
The design of the *Ghost* was inspired by the Boeing B-17 Flying Fortress heavy bomber used in World War II.

HIDE AND SEEK

The **sneaky** *Ghost* and its **attack shuttle**, the *Phantom*, can operate separately, but they work best together, as a **single starship**. This is ideal for its rebel crew, who need **all the options** they can get when **fighting** or **fleeing** the Empire!

THE SHOWDOWN: *GHOST* VS *FALCON*
The *Ghost* may **not** be able to **outrace** the legendary *Millennium Falcon*, but it wins **sizewise**! The *Falcon* is 34m (112ft) long x 25.61m (84ft) wide, but the *Ghost* **punches in** at 43.9 (144ft) long x 34.2m (112ft 2in) wide.

Tell me more!

Hyperdrive

NO TIME TO CHECK THE MAP!
The rebels have escaped Imperial forces many times thanks to Hera **swiftly engaging** the *Ghost*'s hyperdrive. But this gives the navicomputer **no time** to chart a path through hyperspace, so they thank their lucky stars they haven't **run into an asteroid** or **bounced off a supernova** yet!

In numbers

1,025kph (636mph)
Ghost's maximum in-atmosphere speed

360 degrees
Swivel of the *Ghost*'s dorsal turret

100
Model number of VCX-class light freighter

4 personal cabins
On the *Ghost*

1 cockpit seat
For piloting the *Phantom*

Q: What good is the *Phantom* if it has no hyperdrive or shields?
A: A lot! Its maneuverability, small size, and rapid-thrust sub-light engines are **vital** for zipping in and out of **tight squeezes**—something the rebels know a lot about!

181

Fast Facts

CAPTAIN: Han Solo

MANUFACTURER: Corellian Engineering Corporation

WEAPONRY: 2 quad laser cannons, 2 concussion missile launchers, 1 blaster cannon

MODEL: Heavily customized YT-1300f light freighter

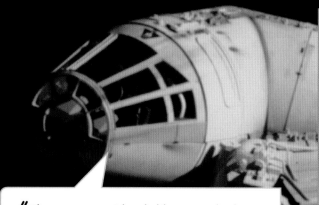

"She may not look like much, but she's got it where it counts, kid."
HAN ON THE *MILLENNIUM FALCON* TO LUKE

Who's who in the crew

The *Millennium Falcon* needs at least two people to fly the ship—a pilot and copilot. But it helps to have extra people on board to man the two gun stations and computers!

HAN SOLO
Owner, captain, gunner, mechanic

LANDO CALRISSIAN
Owner (previous), captain (at times)

CHEWBACCA
Copilot to Han and Lando, mechanic

NIEN NUNB
Copilot to Lando

GENERAL CRACKEN
Gunner (under Lando)

LIEUTENANT BLOUNT
Gunner (under Lando)

LUKE SKYWALKER
Gunner (under Han), passenger (under Han and Lando)

MISSION FILES

1. Smuggling Jabba's illegal goods
Han has to eject the cargo before the Empire boards. ~~FAIL~~

2. Providing transport to Alderaan
Han tries to take Luke and Obi-Wan to Alderaan, but the planet has been destroyed. ~~FAIL~~

3. Rescuing the princess
The crew rescues Leia from the Death Star and the *Falcon* carries her to safety. SUCCESS

4. Battle of Yavin
Piloting the *Falcon*, Han takes Vader out of the battle, while Luke blows up the Death Star. SUCCESS

5. Battle of Endor
Lando flies the *Falcon* to destroy the second Death Star. SUCCESS

Peek behind the scenes
The *Millennium Falcon* went through a late design change, just before filming began. The final shape was inspired by a hamburger and a traditional flying saucer!

A PIECE OF JUNK?

In its long service, the *Millennium Falcon* is many things—**a freighter, a smuggler's vessel, and a warship**. To Han Solo and Chewbacca, it's also **home**... not to mention the **most important starship** in the Rebellion!

TOP 10

NARROW ESCAPES MADE BY THE *FALCON*

1. Being swarmed by TIE fighters.
2. Getting chased by Star Destroyers.
3. Being pulled aboard the Death Star.
4. Crashing into an asteroid.
5. Getting swallowed by a space slug.
6. Being chewed on by mynocks.
7. Having an Imperial tracking device planted on board.
8. Getting boarded by stormtroopers.
9. Being chased by bounty hunters.
10. Zooming through Death Star II.

WOW!...

1,050

The *Falcon's* maximum in-atmosphere speed in kph (652mph)

Q: What is dejarik?

A: The *Millennium Falcon* has a checkered **dejarik (chess) hologame table** that Chewbacca enjoys playing with. The game includes characters of eight different species, including a **Ng'ok, Houjix, Mantellian Savrip, Ghhhk, K'lor'slug, Kintan strider, Monnok,** and **Grimtaash the Molator**.

BEST KNOWN FOR

MAKING THE KESSEL RUN IN LESS THAN 12 PARSECS

The *Millennium Falcon*

STRANGE

...BUT TRUE
Han didn't buy the *Millennium Falcon*. He **won** the ship from **Lando Calrissian**, who **bet** the *Falcon* in a high-stakes game of **Sabacc!**

Top 5

In numbers

3720 to 1
The odds of the *Falcon* safely navigating Hoth's asteroid belt

100 metric tons (220,462lbs)
Cargo capacity

94
The *Falcon's* docking bay number in Mos Eisley

6 passengers
The number who can be comfortably accommodated

5 escape pods
Model CEC Class-1

0.5 hyperdrive class
The *Falcon's* lightspeed rating—twice as fast as most Imperial warships

REALLY?!

The *Falcon's* computer is made of **THREE DROID BRAINS**—an **R3 ASTROMECH**, a **V-5 TRANSPORT DROID**, and a **SLICER DROID!**

Repairs and enhancements

1 ENGINE CHANGE
Allows the *Falcon* to outrun Imperial starships and bulk cruisers.

2 SCANNER-PROOF COMPARTMENTS
Good for hiding people and cargo from Imperial inspections.

3 WEAPONS UPGRADES
Modified laser and blaster cannons to take out pirates and TIE fighters.

4 HYPERDRIVE REPAIR
Gets fixed in Cloud City, enabling the *Falcon* to escape the Empire.

5 NEW SENSOR DISH
To replace the one smashed in the Battle of Endor.

MIGHTY FLEET

With its massive **Star Destroyers**, sleek **shuttles**, and swarming **TIE fighters**, the powerful Imperial Navy is a constant reminder of the Emperor's **iron grip** on the galaxy.

Fast Facts

Imperial ships have names that intimidate, such as *Devastator*, *Avenger*, and *Executor*.

BIGGEST VEHICLE:
Super Star Destroyer

SMALLEST VEHICLE:
Droid starfighter

WEAPONRY:
Turbolasers, ion cannons, tractor beams

Peek behind the scenes
The sound of diving German World War II Stuka bombers inspired the iconic scream of the TIE fighter engine.

WHAT MAKES A STAR DESTROYER?

All Star Destroyers are **gigantic warships** with **pointed hulls**, but that's where their similarities end. The *Acclamator*-class assault ship (1) is mainly a **troop transport**. The *Venator*-class (2) is more heavily armed than the assault ship and is also a **fighter carrier**. The giant *Imperial*-class Star Destroyers (3) are self-contained **mobile bases**, and all are dwarfed by the colossal Super Star Destroyers (4).

1

4

2

3

Q: Where are TIE fighters manufactured?

A: The Empire builds TIE fighters at **Sienar Fleet Systems factories** across the galaxy, including the advanced facility on the **planet Lothal**.

REALLY?!
Only **10 PERCENT** of Imperial Navy cadets **GRADUATE** to become pilots. Their pride in this accomplishment makes them **ARROGANT** and **BOSSY**.

20m (65ft 7in) — Imperial shuttle

9.6m (31ft 6in) — TIE interceptor

9.2m (30ft) — TIE bomber

8.99m (29ft 6in) — TIE fighter

Small but lethal

From the well-armed **TIE interceptor** to the devastating **TIE bomber**, the Imperial Navy uses a range of smaller craft to maintain order in the galaxy.

In numbers

1,600m (5,249ft)
Length of an *Imperial*-class Star Destroyer

1,200kph (745mph)
In-atmosphere speed of a TIE fighter

60
Turbolaser batteries on a Star Destroyer

13
Engine clusters on a Super Star Destroyer

STRANGE

...BUT TRUE
Standard Imperial protocol requires that a Star Destroyer **dump its trash into space**, before jumping to hyperspace.

Star Destroyers carry enough supplies to travel for two years without restocking.

BEST KNOWN FOR

CHASING THE MILLENNIUM FALCON

Imperial Navy

"There's too many of them!"
REBEL PILOT TELSIJ ON THE OVERWHELMING SIZE OF THE IMPERIAL NAVY

WHAT IS THE MOST COMMON SHIP IN THE IMPERIAL NAVY?

A TIE fighter

When the Imperials need to move small cargo, groups of prisoners, or a squad of troops, they use the *Gozanti*-class freighter. Boasting serious firepower, the freighter carries four TIE fighters for protection.

WOW!...

9,700

Stormtroopers stationed on a single Star Destroyer

Q: How does the Emperor travel?
A: Emperor Palpatine uses his own personal **Imperial shuttle**, staffed with Royal Guards and **heavily armed** with **five sets of laser cannons**.

Fast Facts

AFFILIATION: Galactic Empire

ROLE: Planet-smashing battle station

WEAPONRY: Superlaser, turbolasers

DEFENSES: Tractor beams, TIE fighters

STRANGE...

...BUT TRUE
Emperor Palpatine **executes the designer** responsible for the first Death Star's **weak spot**. He then **clones him** and makes him design Death Star II **without the fault.**

WHAT'S IN A NAME?
The first Death Star is given several code names during its construction, including "Ultimate Weapon" and "Sentinel Base."

Those **little robots scuttling** around the first Death Star and Death Star II **aren't vermin**! They're MSE-6 **"mouse droids,"** employed in their hundreds to **keep the floors clean.**

BEST KNOWN FOR

OBLITERATING THE PLANET ALDERAAN

Death Star

DOOMSDAY WEAPONS

Q. What's the size of a small moon and has enough firepower to blast a planet to bits?
A. One of the Empire's **mighty Death Star battle stations**, built to keep rebellious star systems in line—or else!

BATTLE STATIONS!

Both boast massive firepower, but Death Star II has more advanced weaponry • Both carry huge numbers of Imperial Navy, Army, and stormtroopers

"That's no moon. It's a space station."
OBI-WAN KENOBI ON THE DEATH STAR

Death Star		Death Star II
120km (75 miles)	Diameter	160km (99 miles)
Grand Moff Tarkin	Commander	Moff Jerjerrod
342,953	Total crew	637,835
15,000	Turbolaser batteries	30,000
24 hours	Superlaser recharge time	3 minutes
768	Tractor beam emplacements	768

186

GROSS!!

A **DIANOGA SQUID** lurks in the Death Star's garbage compactor. Its usual diet is **ROTTING TRASH**, but Luke looks **PRETTY TASTY**, too!

In numbers

2,471,647 passengers and crew
On Death Star II

7,500 laser cannons
On Death Star II

5,000 ion cannons
On Death Star II

560 internal levels
On Death Star II

357 internal levels
On the first Death Star

DESTROYER OF WORLDS

At the heart of the Death Star lies a **devastating weapon of doom**—the superlaser. Powered by hypermatter reactors, it focuses multiple lasers through massive kyber crystals into one **planet-shattering beam**.

Peek behind the scenes

The sound of the giant **Death Star** ray that blasts Alderaan is taken in part from the buzzing of spaceships in the 1930s Flash Gordon science fiction serials, favorites of George Lucas.

Tell me more!

FATAL FLAWS

Both Death Star battle stations prove to have significant **faults**—and the rebels exploit them! **Luke Skywalker** fires **torpedoes** from his X-wing into an open **exhaust vent** to blow up the first Death Star. Death Star II falls when rebel teams disable its **shield** and explode its **reactor core**.

Q: What is The Disaster?

A: The Disaster is the **destruction of Alderaan**, Princess Leia's homeworld. Grand Moff Tarkin annihilates the planet to demonstrate the Death Star's **terrifying power**. The two-faced Tarkin breaks his promise to Leia to **spare Alderaan** in return for information about a **secret rebel base**.

Top 5

Locations on the Death Star and Death Star II

1 EMPEROR'S THRONE ROOM
Never used on the first Death Star. Evil emperors have little time to sit and give orders.

2 OVERBRIDGE
Command center and commanders' headquarters.

3 SUPERLASER CONTROL STATIONS
Prepare and fire the weapon.

4 DETENTION BLOCKS
Section where prisoners are interrogated and executed.

5 HYPERMATTER REACTORS
Generate huge amounts of power. When these are wiped out, so are the Death Star battle stations!

WOW!...

1,000,000,000,000+

Cost of building a Death Star in galactic credits (one trillion plus)

THE NEW ERA

CHAPTER 5 ▶

REY AND BB-8

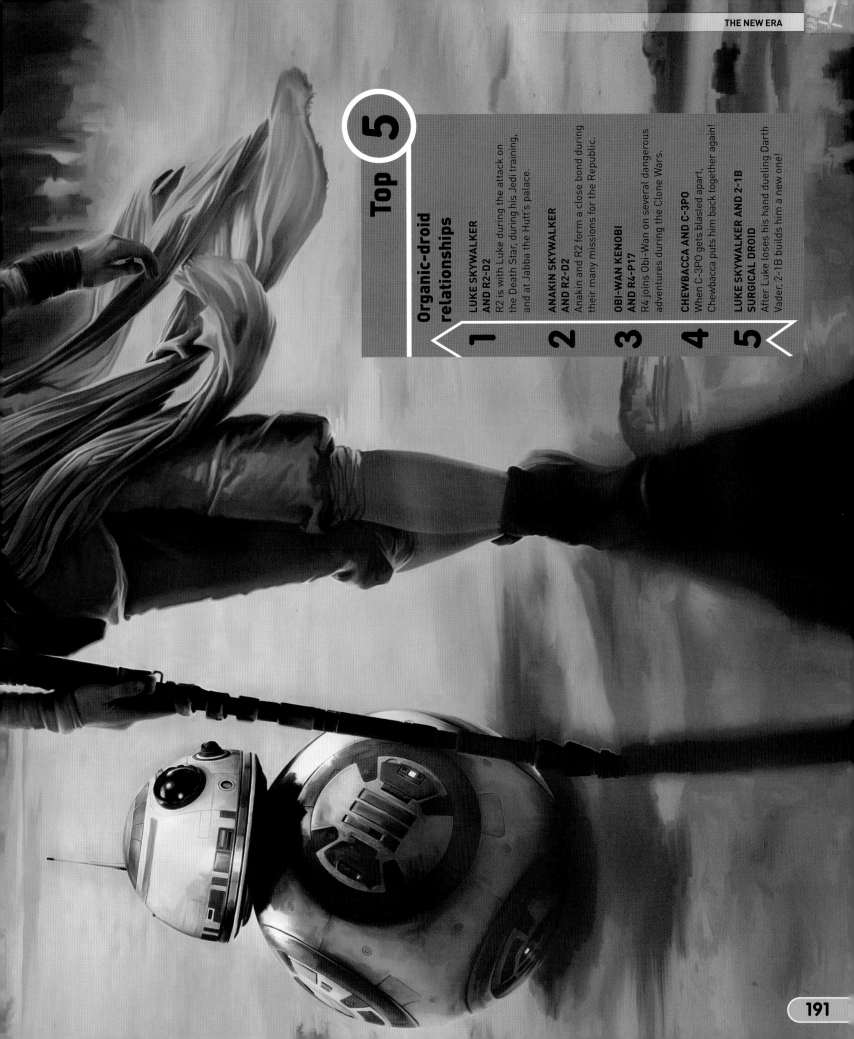

Top 5

Organic-droid relationships

1 LUKE SKYWALKER AND R2-D2
R2 is with Luke during the attack on the Death Star, during his Jedi training, and at Jabba the Hutt's palace.

2 ANAKIN SKYWALKER AND R2-D2
Anakin and R2 form a close bond during their many missions for the Republic.

3 OBI-WAN KENOBI AND R4-P17
R4 joins Obi-Wan on several dangerous adventures during the Clone Wars.

4 CHEWBACCA AND C-3PO
When C-3PO gets blasted apart, Chewbacca puts him back together again!

5 LUKE SKYWALKER AND 2-1B SURGICAL DROID
After Luke loses his hand dueling Darth Vader, 2-1B builds him a new one!

FIRST ORDER STORMTROOPERS

Top ⑤

Worst stormtrooper crimes

1 DESTROYING THE LARS HOMESTEAD
Owen and Baru Lars are ruthlessly executed, and their home is burned to the ground.

2 MASSACRING DEFENSELESS JAWAS
An entire clan of Jawas is wiped out and their sandcrawler base is destroyed.

3 TORTURING HAN SOLO
Han is tortured so that Luke Skywalker senses his pain, and is tricked into coming to Cloud City.

4 OPPRESSING EWOKS ON ENDOR
Stormtroopers clear the forest for the Death Star II's shield generator, uprooting countless Ewoks in the process.

5 BLOWING UP C-3PO
When C-3PO stumbles upon stormtroopers on Cloud City, they blast him to pieces without a second thought.

Top 5

Red lightsaber wielders

1 DARTH VADER
Even when slowed down by his armor, Darth Vader is a truly lethal opponent.

2 DARTH SIDIOUS
When necessary, Sidious can unleash a dark side-fueled frenzy of strikes and slashes.

3 DARTH MAUL
Maul uses his double-bladed lightsaber to create a terrifying vortex of energy!

4 DARTH TYRANUS
Tyranus has spent a lifetime honing his elegant lightsaber dueling skills.

5 ASAJJ VENTRESS
Asajj's power lies in her unique twin blades combined with her ferocious fighting style.

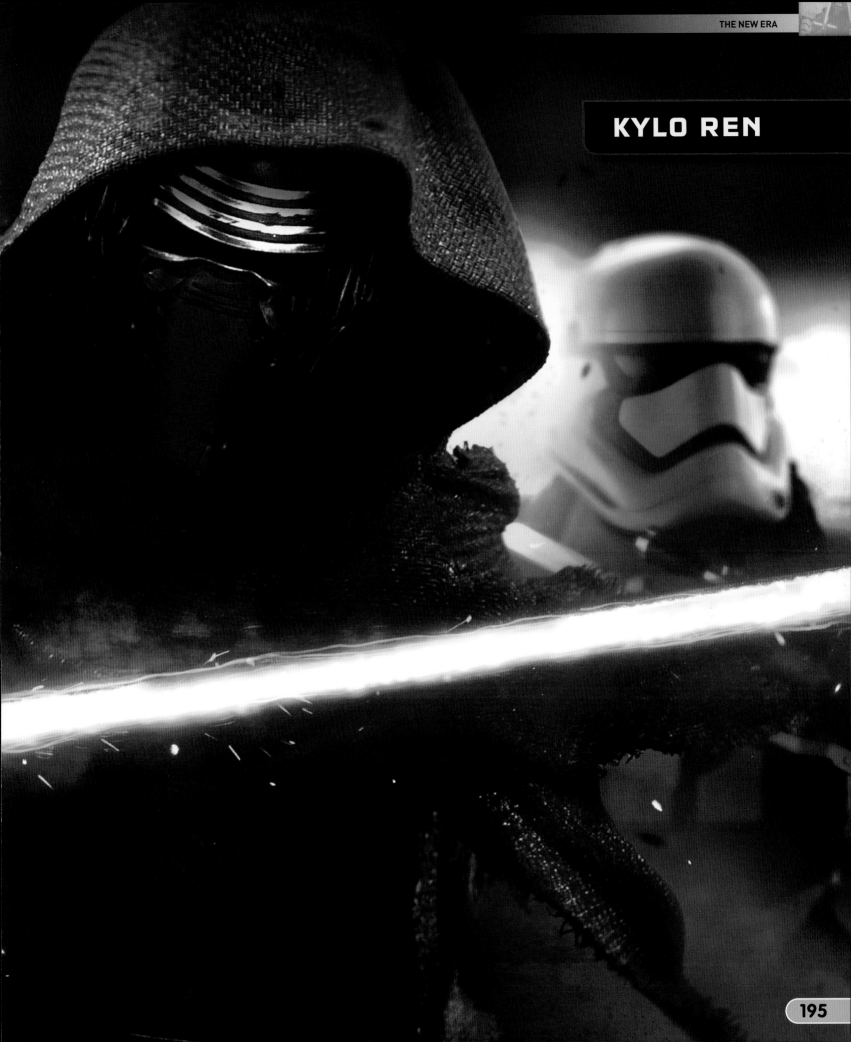

KYLO REN

INDEX

Page numbers in **bold** indicate main entries. Characters are listed according to their most commonly used name, for example Han Solo is under "H" and Asajj Ventress is under "V". Characters whose names usually include a title are listed that way, for example Count Dooku is under "C".

A

A-wing 177
A4-D medical droid 66
Abafar 143
acklay 126
Adi Gallia 8
Admiral Antonio Motti 73
Admiral Gial Ackbar 171
Admiral Wulff Yularen 73
Agent Kallus 35, **74-5**
Ahsoka Tano **14-15**, 125, 143
    and Anakin Skywalker 10, 14, 15, 17, 163
    and Commander Fox 21
    as Fulcrum 14, 26, 74, 180
    and Hondo Ohnaka 95
    and Asajj Ventress 68
aiwhas 139, 156
Ak-rev 113
Aldar Beedo 114
Alderaan 41, 42, 44, 73, 182, 187
Amanaman 105
Amani 160-61
Anakin Skywalker **10-11**, 21, 111
    and Ahsoka Tano 10, 14, 15, 17, 163
    becomes Darth Vader 60-61
    and Count Dooku 59
    and Hondo Ohnaka 95, 125
    Jedi training 12, 13, 31
    and Obi-Wan Kenobi 12, 13
    and Padmé Amidala 10, 153
    podracing 114, 115
    Tusken Raiders 117
    and Yoda 16, 17
    see also Darth Vader
anoobas 124, 125, 150
aqua droid 118
ARC-170 178
Archduke Poggle the Lesser 102, 127, 159
arena beasts **126-7**, 158

Arihnda Pryce 172
Arleil Schous 110
Arok the Hutt 90
ASN courier droid 118
astromech droids 34, 36-7, 48-9, 94, 164, 183
AT-AT walkers 164, 165
Attark the Hoover 125
Aurra Sing 15, 84, 95

B

B2 super battle droid 119
B2-3000 luxury droid 119
bacta 41
Balnab castaways 125
Bane, Cad **86-7**, 163
banshees 138
banthas 117, 132, 134, 150
Barada 104, 145
Baron Papanoida 15
Baron Rudor 31
battle beasts **128-9**
battle droids 64, 65, 102, 119, 128, 158, 159
beasts **122-3**, 150, 187
    arena beasts **126-7**, 158
    battle beasts **128-9**
    beasts of burden **132-3**
    creepy-crawlies **140-41**
    ice beasts **134-5**
    land beasts **142-3**
    sea creatures **130-31**, 161
    space beasts **136-7**
    swamp beasts 166-7
    underground beasts **144-5**
    winged beasts **138-9**
Ben Quadinaros 115
Beru Lars 40, 41
Bespin **168-9**
Bib Fortuna 104, 105, 125
Bith **112-13**
blarths 125

Blizzard Force 164
Blue Shadow Virus 15, 122
Bo-Katan Kryze 92
Boba Fett 43, **84-5**, 86, 105, 145
bogwings 138, 139
Boles Roor 114
Bom Vimdin 111
B'omarr monastery 23
B'omarr monks 151
Boonta Eve Classic Podrace 10, 11, 114-15
Boonta Hestilic Shad'ruu 115
Boss Nass 130
Bossk 86, 105
bounty hunters 92, 150, 155, 182
    Boba Fett 43, **84-5**, 86, 105, 145
    Cad Bane **86-7**, 163
    Castas 122
    Jango Fett 69, **84-5**, 95, 127, 141, 156
Boushh 44, 91
The Box 86
Braconnor Bakiska 110
brain worms 141
brezaks 138, 139
Bubo (Buboicullaar) 104, 124, 125
bucket-heads **78-9**
buzz droids 179

C

C1-10P 118
C-3PO **48-9**, 163
    and Anakin Skywalker 11
    and Cad Bane 87
    and Chewbacca 47, 48
    and the Ewoks 43, 48, 101
    at Jabba's Palace 104, 105, 144
    and the Jawas 108, 109
can-cells 138, 139
Capital City 172, 173
Captain Rex 21, 157
Captain Tarpals 129
carbonite freezing 43, 85, 168
carrier butterflies 138
Castas 122
Cerea 9
Cham Syndulla 27, 74
Chancellor Palpatine 10, 20, 21, 54-5, 86, 87
Chewbacca (Chewie) 34, **46-7**, 169
    and C-3PO 47, 48
    and Jabba the Hutt 44, 45, 91, 105
    Millennium Falcon 182-3
Chief Chirpa 100, 101
Chopper 34, **36-7**, 180
Cikatro Vizago 172
CLE-004 cleaning droid 118
Cleigg Lars 116

clone army 58, 156-7
clone troopers **20-22**, 84, 85, 143, 145, 158
    vehicles and weapons **22-3**
Clone Wars
    and Ahsoka Tano 14
    and Anakin Skywalker 10
    and Asajj Ventress 68
    Battle of Geonosis 158-9
    clone troopers 21, 22, 106
    and Hondo Ohnaka 95
    and Obi-Wan Kenobi 74
    and Palpatine 55
Cloud City 48, 49, **168-9**, 183
colo claw fish 131
Commandant Aresko 31, 77, 79, 172
Commander Cody 13, 20, 21
Commander Fox 21
Commander Gree 20, 21
Concordia 92, 93
Confederacy of Independent Systems 159
convorees 124-5, 138
Corporate Alliance tank droid 119
Coruscant 86, **154-5**
Count Dooku **58-9**
    and Anakin Skywalker 11, 59
    and Asajj Ventress 68
    and bounty hunters 84, 86
    and clone troopers 21
    and Geonosis 159
    and Hondo Ohnaka 95
    and the Trade Federation
crab droid 119
creepy-crawlies **140-41**

D

dactillions 138, 139
Dagobah 16, 17, **166-7**
Darksaber 92
Darth Maul 54, **56-7**, 94
    and Obi-Wan Kenobi 8, 12, 13, 57, 69
Darth Plagueis 54
Darth Sidious **54-5**
    and Anakin Skywalker 61
    apprentices 58, 59, 76
    and Cad Bane 86, 87
    duel with Yoda 17
    Mustafar 162, 163
    Order 66 20
    and the Trade Federation 64
Darth Tyranus 58, 59
Darth Vader **60-61**
    Anakin Skywalker becomes 10, 60-61
    apprentice to Darth Sidious 76
    Battle of Yavin 182
    Force choking 60, 73

freezes Han Solo in carbonite
43, 85
and the Inquisitor 76, 77, 161
and Luke Skywalker 40, 54,
167, 169
Mustafar 163
see also Anakin Skywalker
Dathomir 57, 68
Dazon, Hem 111
Death Star (the first) 54, 72, 73, 78,
182, **186-7**
and Han Solo 42, 43
Luke destroys 40, 41
stolen plans 45, 48
Death Star II 170, 182, **186-7**
Death Watch 32, 33, **92-3**
dejarik 183
Dengar 105
Depa Billaba 29
dewbacks 132, 133, 150
dianoga squid 187
the Disaster 187
Dr. Evazan 110
Dooku's Palace 58
droids 109, **118-9**, 164
astromech 34, 36-7, 48-9, 94,
118, 164, 183
battle 64, 65, 102, 119, 128,
158, 159
courier 118
droideka 119
medical 66, 118
military 126
mining 163
mouse 186
probe 118, 165
protocol 48-9, 65, 118, 119
Separatist droid army 58, 66-7
starfighters 178-9, 184
Droopy McCool 112, 113
Duchess Satine Kryze 13, 92
Dugs 122
duracrete slugs 140
Duros 110
dwarf spider droid 119

E

Ebe E. Endocott 114
Echo 21
Echo Base 164-5
Elan Mak 114
Embo 124
Emperor Palpatine **54-5**, 72, 76
Death Star 186
Imperial Navy 184-5
Imperial Security Bureau 74
Order 66 13
Empire 35, 61 , 78
Empire Day 31

and Endor 170
fall of 40
Grand Moff Tarkin 72-3
Imperial Academy 32, 37, 40,
79, 173
Imperial Navy 184-5
Imperial officers **72-3**, 76, 79
Imperial Security Bureau (ISB)
74, 75
Imperial walkers 100
and Lothal 172-3
weapons 22, 78, 79
Endor 43, 46, 48, **170-71**
Battle of Endor 100-1, 182, 183
eopies 132, 133, 150
Ephant Mon 104
Ephraim Bridger 31
EV-909 supervisor droid 118
Even Piell 8
Ewoks 43, 46, 48, **100-1**, 170-71
exogorth space slugs 136, 137
Ezra Bridger **30-31**, 34, 36, 173, 180
and the fyrnocks 136
and the Inquisitor 76
and Kanan Jarrus 26, 29, 77
and Sabine 32
and Yoda 17

F

falumpasets 128, 129
fambaa 128, 129
"Fiery" Figrin D'an 112
firefighter droid 118
Fives 21
Florrum 94, 95, 143
flying squid 161
Fodesinbeed Annodue 114, 115
the Force 8, 10, 13, 44, 45, 166-7
Force choking 60, 68, 69, 73
Force spirits 16
Form Three 29
Fort Anaxes asteroid 137, 180
frog-dogs 124
Fulcrum 14, 26, 74, 180
fyrnock 136, 137
FX-7 medical assistance droid 118

G

Galactic Empire 35, 61
Empire Day 31
and Endor 170
fall of 40
Grand Moff Tarkin 72-3
Imperial Academy 32, 37, 40, 173
Imperial Navy **184-5**
Imperial officers 72-3, 76
Imperial Security Bureau (ISB)
74, 75
Imperial walkers 100

and Lothal 172-3
weapons 22
Galactic Senate Building 155
Gall Trayvis 33, 74
Gamorrean guards 123
Gardulla Besadii the Elder 10, 11,
90, 91
Gartogg 104
Gasgano 114
Gauron Nas Tal 105
General Cassio Tagge 73
General Cracken 182
General Dodonna 45
General Grievous 13, 15, **66-7**, 123
General Rieekan 45, 164
Geonosians 65, **102-3**, 145, **158-9**
Geonosis 102-3, 126-7, **158-9**
Battle of Geonosis 20, 59,
94, 158
Ghost 34, 176, **180-1**
and Chopper 36, 37, 180
and Ezra Bridger 30, 31, 180
and Hera Syndulla 26, 27, 28,
180, 181
ginnthos 161
Gorga Desilijic Aarrpo 90
Grand Moff Tarkin **72-3**, 76,
172, 187
Greedo 111
gundarks 13, 122
Gungans **106-7**
beasts 128-9, 139
food 140
Naboo 130, 152-3
pets 125
gutkurrs 122
Gwarm 94

H

Han Solo **42-3**
and Boba Fett 85, 105
and Chewbacca 46, 47
and the Death Star 41, 42
is frozen in carbonite 42, 43,
85, 168
on Hoth 165
and Jabba the Hutt 43, 91,
105, 111
Millennium Falcon 42, 137, 182-3
and Princess Leia 43, 45
tauntaun 134, 135
Hera Syndulla **26-7**, 28, 36, 180, 181
Hermi Odle 105
Hesten monkeys 125
Holocron 28
hologame 183
homing spider droid 119
Hondo Ohnaka 59, **94-5**, 125
horaxes 134

Hoth 133, 134-5, **164-5**
Battle of Hoth 45, 164
Hoth asteroid belt 137
Hutt Grand Council 90, 91
Hutts 15, 86, **90-91**, 115

I

ice beasts **134-5**
IG-88 assassin droid 119
IG-RM droids 172
ikopi 142, 143
Iktotchi 9
Imperial Academy 32, 37, 40,
79, 173
Imperial Navy **184-5**
Imperial officers **72-3**, 76, 79
Imperial Security Bureau (ISB) **74-5**
Imperial shuttle 177
Imperial walkers 100
the Inquisitor **76-7**, 173
and Darth Vader 61, 76, 77, 161
and Ezra Bridger 30, 31, 76, 136
and Kanan Jarrus 28, 29
space ships 37, 77
interceptor 176, 177, 178
Ishi Tib 104
IT-0 interrogator droid

J

J-1 proton cannon 119
Jabba the Hutt 86, **90-91**
and Han Solo 43, 85, 105,
135, 182
Jabba's Palace **104-5**, 113, 125
and music 113, 171
pets 123, 124, 125, 144, 145
and Princess Leia 44, 45
Jango Fett 69, **84-5**, 95, 127, 141, 156
Jar Jar Binks **106-7**, 130, 143, 153
Jawas **108-9**, 133, 150
Jaynor 33
Jedi 54, 55, 77, 130
Jedi Knights 8-11, 14-15, 40-41,
58, 59, 94
Jedi Masters **8-9**, 10, 12-13, 15,
16-17, 21, 40-41, 59
Jedi Padawan 10-11, 14-15, 17,
28-31, 40, 58
space ships 177, 178-9
Jedi Archives 76, 87, 156
Jedi High Council **8-9**, 10, 16,
20, 127
Jedi Temple 9, 14, 15, 21, 30, 92, 155
Jesse 21
Jiro 94
Joh Yowza 171
Jundland Wastes 116-17, 150

Editor Ruth Amos
Project Art Editor Toby Truphet
Senior Editor Cefn Ridout
Senior Designers Robert Perry, Anne Sharples
Editors David Fentiman, Julia March
US Editor Allison Singer
Additional design by Owen Bennett, Karan Chaudhary, Chris Gould, Pranika Jain, Simon Murrell, Anna Pond, Clive Savage
Jacket design Toby Truphet
Senior Pre-Production Producer Jennifer Murray
Senior Producer Alex Bell
Managing Editor Sadie Smith
Managing Art Editor Ron Stobbart
Art Director Lisa Lanzarini
Publisher Julie Ferris
Publishing Director Simon Beecroft

Dorling Kindersley would like to thank: Jonathan W. Rinzler, Troy Alders, Pablo Hidalgo, Leland Chee, and Rayne Roberts at Lucasfilm. Many thanks also to Anna Pond and Lynne Moulding for image research; Cole Horton for extra author research; Neha Ahuja and Chitra Subramanyam for design and editorial assistance; and Vanessa Bird for the index. Special thanks to Star Wars fans Luke Harris for the Fan Fact on p17, Joshua Divall for the Fan Fact on p61, and Mark Newbold for the Fan Fact on p91.

In 2014 Lucasfilm reclassified what is considered canon in the Star Wars universe. Star Wars: Absolutely Everything You Need to Know draws mostly upon information from the Expanded Universe that Lucasfilm now considers to be "Legends"–that is, stories beyond the original six films and the TV shows Star Wars: The Clone Wars and Star Wars Rebels.

First American Edition, 2015
Published in the United States by DK Publishing
345 Hudson Street, New York, New York 10014

Page design copyright © 2015 Dorling Kindersley Limited
A Penguin Random House Company
15 16 17 18 19 10 9 8 7 6 5 4 3 2 1
001–197064–Sept/2015

© & TM 2015 LUCASFILM LTD.

A catalog record for this book is available from the Library of Congress.
ISBN 978-1-4654-3785-3

DK books are available at special discounts when purchased in bulk for sales promotions, premiums, fund-raising, or educational use. For details, contact: DK Publishing Special Markets, 345 Hudson Street, New York, New York 10014
SpecialSales@dk.com

Printed in China

A WORLD OF IDEAS:
SEE ALL THERE IS TO KNOW

www.dk.com
www.starwars.com